Everyone is talking about…

Free & Easy Ways to Promote Your Massage, Spa & Wellness Business! Volume 1: Getting Clients (& Keeping Them!)

"I love the goals section. You can't get to where you want to go, unless you know exactly what you want and plot the course to get there. The goal achieving section alone will change your life as well as your business. This book is a MUST HAVE in order to help the more artistic mind, focus, plan and organize."

Lora Condon aka *"The Beauty Buster"*
*Author of **Spa Wars: The Ugly Truth About the Beauty Industry***
www.makeupwithme.com

"I think this is an excellent book for massage, spa and wellness professionals. In fact any health care professional could use it. I love the worksheets and examples. They are a great way to get your thoughts and goals down and create a working model. If you've bought this book, I think you have a winner."

Dr. Dennis Buckley, DC
*Author of **SCORE: Student Chiropractors On Road to Excellence***
www.Health-Advantage.net

"Bring new clients through the door and learn to keep them, with Felicia's tips in 'Free & Easy Ways to Promote Your Massage, Spa & Wellness Business.' This book describes achievable goals in an easy to follow step-by-step fashion, so therapists can master each strategy towards building a more successful practice."

Tina Allen
Founder
Liddle Kidz Foundation
www.LiddleKidz.com

"Whether you are just starting out or have been in business for decades and would like more clients, this is the book for you! Felicia has created a book that will absolutely elevate your marketing skills and you WILL make more money. Her valuable experience and wisdom shows up in every word. I highly recommend that you have this book in your library, you will use it over and over again."

Shelene Taylor
*Author of **Massage Business Success!***
www.IAmBiz.com

"This book is a fabulous resource for spa owners, managers and employees as well as solo operators. By using the techniques, tips and scripts to get and keep new clients, your business and staff will make more money while providing a more rewarding experience for your customers."

Allan Share
President
Day Spa Association/International Medical Spa Association
www.DaySpaAssociation.com

"Felicia Brown surely has shared from experience and wisdom a great guideline for any therapist that provides clear and concise information. I specifically appreciate the goal setting. Simple, easy, baby steps to get you where you want to go."

Gloria Coppola, LMT
*Author of **Both Ends of the Rainbow: Lomilomi ~ A Healing Journey***
www.GloriaCoppola.com

"Full of practical advice and tips that any business can begin using tomorrow. I especially loved the idea that your e-mail signature is a marketing opportunity-free and easy to use!"

Patti Biro
Patti Biro and Associates
www.pattibiro.com

"Felicia Brown combines experience, insight and business-savvy in her first book. A delightful read, the book provides effective tactics, starting with coaching the reader to identify her/his own passions and forming a vision of the ideal client.

The advice is pragmatic filled with exercises and sample scripts for the reader to flatten her/his learning curve and get on quickly with the business of building a clientele. I found the section on working with social media particularly helpful, and applaud the section on working first with PYK...People You Know."

Donald Quinn Dillon, RMT
*Author of **Massage Therapist Practice: Start – Sustain - Succeed***
www.MassageTherapistPractice.com

"Felicia's book is full of practical, affordable tips to gain new massage clients and get more business from current clients. In addition to tons of good information, Felicia offers real-life scripts and workbooks so the reader can go through his/her own process and customize marketing tactics for each unique situation. This book is a "must-have" for any individual massage therapist or spa owner wanting to grow their business."

Nancy Griffin
Principal
Contento Marketing Group
www.contentomarketing.com

"This book is full of some fantastic, achievable ideas that will most certainly provide you with a strong return on investment. I have done many of these exact concepts while building *The Boston Bodyworker*. And I will tell you that they work IF you are willing to put forth the effort. If you are serious about having a rewarding career in massage, *invest in yourself* by purchasing this book."

Drew Freedman
Principal
The Boston Bodyworker, LLC & Let's Get Clinical
www.BostonBodyworker.com

"Felicia demonstrates joy in her profession and loves to aid those who seek her counsel to take their businesses and organizations to the next level. Her words, ideas, persistence and work model ensure that you will get the job done. LmtPro purchased twenty copies of her book, and plans to distribute them to our community for gainful insight, practical advice and motivation for business growth. We highly recommend Felicia and her book because of her service, passion, friendliness and professionalism."

Selo Alkaranfil
LMT Pro
www.LMTPro.com

"Felicia Brown is the best marketing coach in the business. I highly recommend her **Group Marketing Coaching Program** as well as her other products and classes. You will earn back a lot more than you spend for any of them and have a much more successful practice or business as a result."

Ryan Hoyme, *AKA "The Massage Nerd"*
www.MassageNerd.com

Every Touch Marketing

Free & Easy Ways to Promote Your
Massage, Spa or Wellness Business

Volume 1: Getting New Clients
(& Keeping Them!)

FELICIA BROWN

Other Titles and Products by Felicia Brown

BOOKS
Reflections of My Heart: A Poetic Journey of Love, Life, Heartbreak & Healing
Contributing Author of *Thank God I…Volume 3*

E-BOOKS
How to Get New Clients
Getting Clients to Rebook
Upselling and Upgrading
Retailing for Massage, Spa & Salon Pros
Successful Event Planning Guide

HOME STUDY PROGRAMS
Smart Spa Marketing
Every Touch Marketing 6 Week Home Study Course
Every Touch Marketing 12 Week Intensive Home Study Course

CDs
Goal Setting: Create Success for Your Life and Business
Just Breathe: Guided Meditations for Inner Peace

ISBN: 1482393956
ISBN-13: 978-1482393958

DEDICATION

To the thousands of massage therapists, spa professionals and healing artists who nurture, help and heal their clients through every touch.

CONTENTS

ACKNOWLEDGMENTS

They say it takes a village to raise a child. Likewise it takes a village to help any person, business or project succeed. Though there are probably hundreds of people I could thank for contributing to my success in business and in writing this book, I would be remiss if I did not at a minimum acknowledge by name a few folks who have profoundly helped and influenced me.

Thank you to Carol Houlihan Brown aka "Buttercup, the Book Doula" for helping me birth this baby book; David Kent for inspiring me to create my own educational products; Dr. Dennis Buckley for helping me aim for completion rather than perfection; Shelene Taylor for encouraging me to reach my full potential.

Thank you to editors Karen Menehan of **Massage Magazine**, "my angel" Leslie Young of **Massage and Bodywork**, and Cherie Sohnen-Moe (plus several others) from **MTJ** for giving me numerous opportunities to share my ideas with the massage therapy world; authors Laura Allen, Don Dillon, Mark Beck, Dan Clements & Tara Gignac, Debra Koerner, Meagan Holub, and John Castagnini for inviting my contributions to their books.

Thank you for the amazing cover design and graphic help – not to mention patience, encouragement and quick turnaround - from Imran Khan of Creative Klub (www.CreativeKlub.com). I am also very thankful for the beautiful head shot/photograph for the back cover and "About the Author" section from Shad Hills. The timing and intention were perfect and more accurately reflect my humorous or playful nature, young spirit and "inner beauty."

Thank you also to Dr. Matthew Norton, Celia Bucci, Kathleen Gramzay and Susan Salvo for ongoing moral support and advice about the ups and downs of writing; to Allan Share and Don Dillon for helpful and spot-on feedback about how to make my "baby" better; to Kathy Howard for helping me improve marketing materials for the book; and to Selo Alkaranfil of LMTPro.com for his enthusiastic and advance PR and book promotions.

I also want to thank everyone who's invited me to teach and speak around the US, Canada and abroad. Each of these forums has provided me with countless ideas, opportunities, and inspirations for my classes, coaching and writing. Thank you to the *American Massage Therapy Association, AMTA-NC, Associated Bodywork and Massage Practitioners,* the *Day Spa Association,* the *International Pedicure Association, Northwestern Health Sciences University, Ryan Hoyme & The Massage Nerd Show, Spa Wellness & Quality Forum, Questex Media/IECSC, PremiereShows,* the *World Massage Conference (Eric Brown, Melanie Hayden & Scott Dartnall)* and the *World Massage Festival* ; and my thousands of students and clients for making my "job" rewarding every day.

I'd especially like to thank my friends at One Concept - Scott Dartnall, Lorna Pasinato, Robyn Donovan-Green, Monica Pasinato-Forchelli, and Angie Patrick - who put on the *American Massage, Chiropractic, Acupuncture & Spa Conferences* and the *Canadian Massage & Chiropractic Conference.* By allowing me to host the *Pre-Conference Broadcast Series* for these events, you've provided an incredible venue for me to get to know the most talented educators in these industries. I am forever grateful for the opportunity to be a part of what you do.

Thanks most of all to the friends who love me no matter what. You should know who you are but thank you to Susan Price, James Moore, Sharon Swift, Cathy & Bailey Jordan, Jed Corman, Angie Dubis, Mike Davis, Ken Loftis, Ben Owen and the entire "old" Jaycee crew/MUSEPers.

Finally, I owe a depth of gratitude to my husband, David, for his unconditional support and acceptance of all that I am and for being an unwavering fan, friend and partner in life.

Namaste, y'all.

FOREWORD

Welcome to *Free & Easy Ways to Promote Your Massage, Spa & Wellness Business: Volume 1 – Getting New Clients (& Keeping Them!)*. I'm a licensed massage therapist and have been in practice since 1994. Like many who are reading this book, I started out working as an independent contractor for other people's businesses for a couple of years. Then one day I realized, "You know what? I'm too hard-headed to do it other people's way. I have my own ideas and really need to be in charge!" So I went out and started my own practice, *Balance Massage Therapy* – or just *Balance* for short.

I was the only therapist in the practice for the first two or three months. Then, because I had a plan and vision for a group practice, I added four therapists who rented space from me. Within a few months, we were so busy we couldn't handle it alone so we added a few more independent contractors to take our overflow. The business continued to grow and grow and grow.

Over the next several years, we added additional space, hired more massage therapists as well as estheticians, nail technicians and support staff - and became a full-fledged day spa. Though we certainly had our share of ups and downs along the way, when I sold the spa in 2005, there were fifty people working for me and the spa itself was doing close to *two million dollars a year in sales* – quite a ways from where we started! Together, the staff and I grew and sustained *Balance* using the same techniques and philosophies that I share with my students and coaching clients today.

To be completely transparent, I also have to say that I've had my share of ups and downs in business, including what many people would call a failure. Several years after I sold the first spa, I opened another spa (*Inspire*) as something of a knee-jerk reaction to a need and opportunity that arose fairly quickly. It (the spa) was a beautiful place but one that was victim to poor timing. We opened in July of

2008, just before the big banking/real estate crash and economic meltdown that followed. Additionally, opening and owning a second spa was not something I truly *wanted* to do but rather something I was willing and able to do – a key difference from my first practice and spa. As a result of this killer combination, I closed *Inspire* after less than a year with severe financial consequences. (You can read more about that in *Thank God I…Volume 3*)

Why do I share that here? Because it's part of my story – and part of my overall success. The lessons I learned from that "failure" were invaluable to my current businesses (my coaching business and my ever-growing group massage practice/yoga studio) and to my overall outlook on life. I also share it because I want you to know that regardless of where you are in your business progress and profits, I can relate, understand and offer experienced, relevant, compassionate advice and help. I want you to know that I have survived and thrived – and that you can too☺

*****

In the years since I sold my first spa, I have shared countless marketing tips for massage, spa and wellness professionals in my classes, email newsletters, blogs, and social media sites because I *love* helping people succeed, especially those who choose to touch, help and heal others through their work. Even more, I get a real kick out of providing people with new ways to have fun *and* make more money while building strong relationships with their clients of the past, present and future. I hope this book will be a resource you use to do so again and again.

This book is focused on two primary topics and sections – **Attracting New Clients** and **Keeping New Clients Through Rebooking** – as they are the backbone of what most service professionals need to focus on when planning to market themselves. However, the first chapter **Marketing: A New Definition** provides a clear overview of my definition of marketing as well as solid base of marketing wisdom and principles to keep in mind as you read and apply the other tips and techniques in the book. I suggest you read it before moving on to the rest of the text.

So get ready to dive in to this collection of free, easy, affordable and effective marketing strategies, techniques and tips. You're on your way to learning new ways of "touching" people positively, getting them into your office and winning their business and loyalty again and again.

Enjoy the book and feel free to email me with own stories and successes for possible inclusion in a future addition so others can learn from *your* wisdom and experiences. And if you want to get more in-depth marketing education and support, please consider enrolling in a future class (live or online), purchasing a Home Study Course or scheduling some one-on-one coaching sessions. You'll find more information at www.Spalutions.com and www.EveryTouchMarketing.com. You can also join our Facebook group for more marketing resources, tips and discussions at https://www.Facebook.com/groups/EveryTouchMarketing/

To your success!

Felicia Brown
Business & Marketing Coach
Speaker, Educator and Author
www.Spalutions.com
www.SmartSpaMarketing.com
www.EveryTouchMarketing.com

1 MARKETING: A NEW DEFINITION

Introduction

Before we move any further, I think it is important to share my definition of marketing. Simply put, I believe marketing is everything that "touches" (or makes an impression on) a client or prospect and causes them to want to do business with you for the first time or the next time. Hence the brand name of my growing collection of marketing tools, inspiring products and coaching programs. Of course in the case of negative touches and impressions, which I call anti-marketing, they may cause people to do business with you for the last time or perhaps not at all! Thus marketing is everyone's job.

It's important for you to recognize that marketing isn't just about having a brochure, website or expensive ads. These "touches" are the factors that cause people to entrust their body, wellness and welfare into your hands an hour or session at a time. It is imperative that you think about what you're doing,

> "Marketing is too important to be left to the marketing department."
>
> **David Packard**

saying, and being out there in the world because it all "touches" the people who will become or refer your future clients. Taken even further, the impressions you make may also affect the ability of your clients to benefit or heal via the treatments you provide.

As a Certified Guerilla Marketing Coach, I've also been trained to teach others how to use their time, energy, imagination and current resources to increase sales, profits and growth in a business. ("Guerilla Marketing" is a phrase coined by Jay Conrad Levinson, author of *Guerilla Marketing* and many other books on marketing.)

Thus the majority of information shared in this book is about free or affordable opportunities, ideas and tools to promote your practice or business, set yourself apart, reach new clients and build rapport with existing clients. The opportunities are really limitless!

By looking at marketing through this new lens and thinking of the way you impact people in all that you do, it should begin to be clear to you that you are immersed in marketing <u>every single day</u>. It starts from the moment you wake up and decide what kind of day you're going to have. It continues when you leave your house and speak to the cashier at Starbucks or the grocery store and continues with the way you answer your phone or respond to client messages throughout the day. Every smile, sentence and moment of interaction you have with others is and can be a marketing vehicle for your practice whether you like it or not. Today's successful practitioner and business person not only realizes this but takes every opportunity to send the right message and intention out into the world.

Let's take a look at some key principles and ideas that will help you create a strong foundation and plan for your success before trying any of the promotions in the following chapters.

Passion: "Do What You Love"

Plain and simple it is vital to love what you do in your massage, spa or wellness career in order to be a success. I also recommend doing only the services or techniques you truly enjoy. Even if you've got certification in a particular modality or are capable of providing a particular service, if you don't like what you are doing, it can turn your day into a real drag. It would be worthwhile to do an assessment of the different services or techniques you offer to make sure they are all a good fit for your current practice.

> "Nothing great in the world has ever been accomplished without passion."
>
> **Hebbel**
> **(German poet)**

This holds true for the types of equipment, products or continuing education you choose to spend your time and money on. Recently I was contemplating taking a reflexology certification class as several of my regulars had asked me about the work (and I needed to get some CE credits.) I did some research, found a reflexology class in my area and all but signed up for it when I realized I really don't enjoy doing foot massage that much. So why in the world would I add that service to my menu of offerings? Needless to say, I didn't take the class and made friends with a reflexologist in town that I could refer my clients to instead. Now, a few years later, I have reflexologists in my own business.

My advice to anyone who wants to have a long-term career is to find your niche –the work that you are the best at and LOVE doing. Then determine the environment you are most happy working in be it your own office, in a spa or medical office, doing outcalls or just part-time out of your house. If you truly love going to work every day like I do, it will be much easier to put in the time to promote yourself, share enthusiasm for what you do and find success in your profession.

> "If you are not doing what you love, you are wasting your time."
>
> **Billy Joel**

Likewise, when looking at new promotions or marketing ideas to try, think about what you really enjoy or excel at doing. If you love to write, then creating a client newsletter or penning articles for a local magazine makes a lot of sense. By contrast, if you are terrified of public speaking or being in front of a crowd, look for alternative ways to promote yourself, at least for the moment.

In other words, make your marketing decisions and other additions based on your likes, dislikes, strengths and weaknesses rather than what you think you "should do" or what everyone else seems to be doing. If you're having fun, it shows and people will be attracted to you because of your passion, enthusiasm and energy. If you're not enjoying your time and journey at work, your clients probably won't either. Unfortunately for all, that is a recipe for lose-lose rather than win –win!

Unique Offering, Brand or Identity

Building on the idea of doing what you love and enjoy, a couple of questions to ask yourself to improve your marketing results are:

"What do I sell?"

"What do my clients buy from me?"

or perhaps more importantly

"What do I do best?"

The answers may seem simple on the outside such as "I give facials"

> "My greatest strength is common sense. I'm really a standard brand - like Campbell's tomato soup or Baker's chocolate."
>
> **Katharine Hepburn**

or "I help people relax." But if you aren't sure of how to answer these, another option is to survey your best or ideal clients with questions like:

"Why did you choose me as your massage therapist/esthetician/acupuncturist?"

"What are the primary results or benefits your receive from getting treatments from me and/or that are the most helpful to you?"

"What do you tell others about me or why they should try me out?"

The answers may surprise you but will provide some incredible insights into how you are different from others in your field and what you need to focus on to attract more of your ideal clients.

As all areas of the massage, spa and wellness industry continue to add schools, there are more and more related practitioners and businesses around that offer a similar range of services as one another. Thankfully, as the number of practitioners continues to grow, more and more new business/employment opportunities and additional client types that emerge.

Finding your piece of success in any field requires that you stake a claim on your individual specialties and niches. This is where redefining, specializing or focusing in on particular kinds of groups, problems or techniques will come in to play. In some cases, broadening what you do in terms of adding additional services or modalities, session times, or products can also help

> "Your premium brand had better be delivering something special, or it's not going to get the business."
>
> **Warren Buffett**

you focus on a particular niche, such as providing massage for second shift workers who want to receive services after 11 PM when they get off work. In turn, these changes should help you to find some specific focal points for your marketing.

And if you are called to do so, you can translate your niche, specialty or brand into a short tagline or slogan that quickly and clearly communicates what you do best to your clients and audience.

Here are some sample tag lines from other industries:

- **Quality is Job One (Ford)**

- **Time to make the donuts (Dunkin' Donuts)**

- **Say it with flowers (FTD)**

- **When you care enough to send the very best (Hallmark)**

The one for my practice is…

"Massage therapy for pain relief, stress reduction and a happier life"

From my former spas…

"Is there Balance in your life?" (Balance Day Spa)

"Are you ready to be inspired?" (Inspire Skin and Body)

What do you want to say about your business, results or reputation?

_____

_____

_____

_____

_____

_____

_____

_____

_____

_____

_____

_____

Goals

Let's jump right in and get you on your way to achieving your professional and financial goals! We have to start by getting a clear picture of exactly what your goals are in order to chart a path or plan for achieving them. My coaching clients hear this all the time but it is SO important for your success. When you know exactly what you want, doors will open, the right people or circumstances will appear to help you achieve your goals.

Without goals, you may find yourself (or your staff) sitting at your desk or computer, or in your treatment room, with no clients, nothing else on your schedule and wondering what to do with the time. You **know** - and perhaps they know - that you should be doing *something* to help your business grow. *But what?*

Creating short-term and long-term goals gives you a foundation and vision that can help you shape our plans for the year, day, and even moment. Defining and following goals

> "Our goals can only be reached through a vehicle of a plan, in which we must fervently believe, and upon which we must vigorously act. There is no other route to success."
>
> **Pablo Picasso**

also helps determine the actions and steps to take to move faster towards the success we want and deserve. Whether you are striving to see a specific number of clients, make a certain amount of income, or even graduate from a particular school or program, goal setting is a critical piece of your foundation and success. And while I could probably write an entire book on the subject of how and why to set goals, there are two or three key points that matter the most.

First, you must know what you want to accomplish in your business or practice so you understand (and get excited about) why you're taking the actions you're taking each day or week to connect with new clients. If you don't have a clear picture of and passion for

> **"If you don't know where you are going, you might wind up someplace else."**
>
> **Yogi Berra**

why you are promoting yourself, then it can become quite a chore indeed!

For most of you reading this book, your main goal will likely be something like "to get more clients" or "to make more money." You may also have some other related goals that you want to declare such as "opening my own office" or "getting certified in Waterless Spa Treatments." Think about what is most important to you and your career right now.

Second, you must determine *as exactly as possible* what you are aiming to achieve professionally. That means determining *exactly* how many new clients you want to bring in or *exactly* how much more money you want to make than you are making right now. You also want to make sure these goals are attached to a definite time-line or deadline and that they are realistic and attainable. We call these SMART goals – Specific, Measurable, Attainable, Realistic and Time-sensitive.

Let me give you an example of what I mean by looking at the basic goal of making more money and seeing more clients.

Jennifer is currently seeing an average of two clients a day, three days a week. She charges $60 a session and works 50 weeks a year.

2 clients x 4 days a week x 50 weeks = 400 clients a year.
400 clients x $60 = $24,000 gross revenue in a year

Jennifer's goal is to double her business and see four clients a day four days a week fifty weeks a year by the end of the next twelve months. She has chosen December 31, 2014 as her deadline for this goal.

4 clients x 4 days a week x 50 weeks a year = 800 clients annually by 12/31/2014
800 clients x $60 = $48,000 gross revenue per year by 12/31/2014

If Jennifer is willing to dedicate herself to taking action daily to reach new clients and to promote herself in a way that creates credibility, trust and rapport, she can most likely meet her goal.

Once you have decided on *your* goals, put them in writing and take time to share your thoughts with your spouse, colleagues, clients, business partners and/or staff. By letting people know what it is you seek to achieve, you will be more likely to have support and perhaps even collaboration on getting your goals met. This is also a great way to get feedback on how you are promoting yourself now and to get additional ideas from your supporters. Take the ideas that they have along with your own and create an action plan for turning your goals into reality.

After your goals and initial action plan are set and written, make sure to review and revise them regularly. Keep track of how you are doing each day, week or month so you can see how close you are to getting what you want. This regular review can also help you keep track of what actions are bringing you closer to your goal so you can continue to do more of what is working well and get rid of the tasks that are not effective.

> **"You need to overcome the tug of people against you as you reach for high goals."**
>
> **George S. Patton**

Of course, if you need to change your goals or deadlines as you work towards achieving them, that's totally fine. In fact, that's exactly why a regular review is part of the goal setting process.

What are some of your goals? Whatever you choose, it's important that you not worry about what someone else's goals are, or think your goals aren't big enough. Your goals should make you feel good, inspired and excited. **And let me stress this point:** Your goals should be what <u>you</u> want and are passionate about, **not** what someone else wants for you or thinks you should have, be or do.

Take a moment to think about your top success goals for your marketing, your business or your career. As you do this it is important to remember that your definition of success and the related goals are very personal. Write down your top two to three professional goals being as specific as possible, <u>giving each goal a deadline</u> and making them as measurable as possible.

Sample Goals

1) *I want to pay myself $40,000 a year by 12/31/15*

2) *I want to reach gross sales of $125K a year by 12/31/15*

3) *I want to consistently have 20 repeat clients a week by 6/30/15*

_____

_____

_____

Select your most important goal and write it below:

_____

Now that you have your main goal determined, how do you start making progress decide what actions or steps to take towards achieving it? The first step is to make a list of the various actions that need to happen to begin making progress.

Begin by writing down all the ways you could move closer toward your desired goal. If there were no obstacles at all, what would or could you do to move toward achieving it? For example, if your main goal is to find a new office, you might list things like determining the area you'd like the office to be in; making a list of all the "must-haves" the office needs such as on-street parking or a private entrance; hiring a realtor; etc.

_____

_____

_____

_____

_____

_____

Using what you've written above, fill in the goal achievement timeline to get a sense of when you'll schedule or do each activity and step.

In 1 week, I will have done the following toward my goal.

_____

In 2 weeks, I will have done the following toward my goal.

_____

In 3 weeks, I will have done the following toward my goal.

_____

In 4 weeks, I will have done the following toward my goal.

_____

_____

In 5 weeks, I will have done the following toward my goal.

_____

_____

In 6 weeks, I will have done the following toward my goal.

_____

_____

In 7 weeks, I will have done the following toward my goal:

_____

_____

In 8 weeks, I will have done the following toward my goal:

_____

_____

In 9 weeks, I will have done the following toward my goal.

_____

_____

In 10 weeks, I will have done the following toward my goal.

_____

_____

In 11 weeks, I will have done the following toward my goal:

_____

_____

In 12 weeks, I will have done the following toward my goal:

_____

_____

_____

*****

If you have trouble prioritizing what actions to take on a daily or weekly basis, try this. As you work on your "to do" list, consider what tasks will likely bring in a client or revenue and *do those first.*

> "Setting goals is the first step in turning the invisible into the visible."
>
> **Tony Robbins**

One other suggestion for success in goal achievement is to remember a big goal you previously achieved such as graduating from school, organizing a large event like a wedding, or training for a marathon. Though the completion of the event or past goal is what is likely clearest in your mind now, think back to the many steps you had to take to get the end result.

An example from my own life:

In 2011, I participated in my first triathlon, an accomplishment that took a lot of preparation. I started by – gulp - setting the goal of completing a triathlon. Next I began looking for events that could be a good fit for me in terms of distance, location and date. A third step was committing to the event by officially registering for it and telling others of my plan.

After I made the commitment to do it, I then had to establish a training regimen and set aside time in my schedule to work on each part of the discipline (swimming, biking and running) leading up to the event. I also had to acquire some new equipment and supplies as well as to get some instruction in the areas where I had less knowledge. Additionally, I took time to research and read about improvements I could make in my diet, recovery strategies and a variety of training techniques. Then finally, I had to go through the competition itself.

Each step of the way - whether on the road, in the pool or in my daily life - took me closer to the eventual finish of that first event. It took quite a bit of preparation, focus, courage and at times, sacrifice, to make it happen. But by focusing on the challenge in front of me rather than the enormity of what seemed impossible, I was able to get through it injury-free. As a bonus, I actually enjoyed myself enough to make triathlons an ongoing hobby and challenge for myself. At this writing I've completed seven and a number of other events!

Striving for and eventually attaining this goal helped me gain greater focus and courage in my businesses and life. Think about a past personal goal that really motivated you - and brainstorm about how you can harness that same level of focus and energy into growing your current practice, spa or clinic!

_____

_____

_____

_____

_____

_____

Your Ideal Clients

Much like doing work that you love and specialize in, to make your marketing effective you'll also want to narrow down the specific groups of people who will most benefit from what you do - and with whom you will enjoy working. Making these changes allows every day and session to be a joy. If you're like me, your ideal clients educate, energize and enthuse you in a way you never expected.

Though many of us would say "My ideal client is someone who can afford my services" there is a lot more to what makes up the picture of our truly ideal clients. Doesn't it sound better to help people who not only can pay for our work, but whom we also love to see?

In my practice, many folks have been coming to me for over a decade, so there is a level of understanding, trust and friendship between us that would be nearly impossible for any of us to replace easily. With that trust and level of understanding, the new clients they refer to me are usually a perfect fit and enhance my practice in the same kinds of ways my long-time regulars do.

To build a following of your own ideal clients, start by determining: who they are; the positive qualities they possess; the benefits or results they are seeking; and what they have in common with one another. Create a clear picture of your ideal client with a persona or short, descriptive narrative describing them. This can even be a wish list of qualities - for each ideal client profile or type.

For example, my ideal massage client persona on the following page is very specific, detailed and descriptive.

My ideal clients are intelligent, genuinely nice, positive-minded people who enjoy life, learning new things and getting a great massage. They value getting weekly or monthly massages for stress reduction, pain relief and pure enjoyment. They are compassionate, understanding and loyal to those who meet their needs, win their trust and gain their friendship.

Though my ideal clients are generally healthy, they want to learn more about preventive care and improving their general wellness. They are moderately physically active to athletic (ex: running, golfing, tennis, Pilates and yoga) and appreciate how our work together plays a part in their overall fitness and well-being. They are also committed to taking an active role in their health and believe that getting regular massage is a vital part of that.

My ideal clients live within a five mile radius of my office and are between forty and eighty in age. They're well-established in their careers as executives, professionals, or entrepreneurs; comfortably retired; or home-makers and have flexible schedules, preferring appointments between 10 AM and 5 PM Monday through Friday or the occasional Saturday.

My ideal clients enjoy some conversation, are open-minded, and think of me as a professional and equal. They also appreciate "the good life" — travel, good food, wine, spas etc., but are down to earth, kind, friendly and generous. They refer freely, tip well, arrive on time and are a joy to work with in every session. Most of all they appreciate me as much as I appreciate them!

I used this information in one very successful promotion I did in which I requested referrals *for ideal clients* from my own massage clients (more on this later). Specifically, I asked them to introduce me to people who were a good fit for my hours of operation, prices, location and personality. These potential new clients would be seeking massage on weekly to monthly basis from a practitioner who would get to know them, their preferences and concerns, and provide them with solutions for stress management, pain relief and relaxation in a private, comfortable, quiet and unrushed environment. I'll

> "Do what you do so well that they will want to see it again and bring their friends."
>
> **Walt Disney**

share the exact particulars of the promotion later in the book but will say here that it was one of the most successful and profitable I've ever done.

Take time now to determine exactly who *your* ideal client is. Spend a few moments reflecting before answering the questions on the next page to learn exactly who you are want to attract to your business. Start with the first four to get clear on the kinds of people that need and want your services. Answer as many of the additional questions as possible to get a deeper understanding of who these clients are as individuals as well as how and where you might find and reach them. Then write your own ideal client description(s) or wish list(s).

Once you've figured out who it is you are trying to attract to your practice, you will naturally begin to find opportunities to find and meet these people and move closer to your goals. It's amazing what getting clarity in these two areas (goals and ideal clientele) can do to propel your business forward.

In the next chapter, we're going to talk about how to find these new ideal clients, market(s) or ideal clientele. You can also make use of the client survey in the **Free Online Resources** (see the *Resources & Free Offers* section at the back of the book for details on getting these) to learn more about your current clients (how they are alike/different in their needs and wants of your business). The better you know your existing and potential ideal clients, the better you can serve their needs and create experiences that wow them.

Ideal Client Profile Questionnaire

1) Who is most likely to be interested in my services and products?

2) What problems are they trying to solve (or experiences are they seeking)?

3) How did they get these problems?

4) How can I help them with their problems (or the experiences they seek) through my services or products?

5) What activities do they participate in?

6) Where do they live?

7) What are their personalities or temperaments like?

8) How old or young are they?

9) What do they have in common with each other or with me?

10) What do they do for a living?

11) What do they do in their free time?

12) Which stores and businesses do my target audience members most often visit?

13) What magazines, newspapers, etc., do my target audience members read?

14) What are people saying about how my services, expertise or business solved their problem or met their needs?

Ideal Client Description or Wish List:

_____

_____

_____

_____

_____

_____

_____

_____

_____

_____

_____

_____

_____

_____

_____

_____

_____

_____

Once you have determined your ideal clients, with each promotion you'll want to clarify a specific goal for the promotion and exactly which groups of ideal clients you're trying to reach. Understanding why they'd be interested in that service or offer and how will it help them will improve your results and help you all get what you want.

As you go through the process of understanding your ideal clients and creating promotions just for them, you will also likely determine there are some clients in your practice that don't "fit" you anymore. They may be overly needy, difficult or individuals you would simply prefer not to see anymore. Take this time to begin thinking about an exit strategy for the relationship so you can make room for more of the people you **do** adore working with.

A few things to consider:

- *Is there a technique, modality, product line or type of work that would benefit them more than what you offer?*
- *Is there a practitioner with whom they would get along better or whose personality or style could be a better fit?*
- *Is there a graceful way to adjust your schedule by enrolling in a class or taking a new day off that coincides with their preferred appointment time that will help you ease the transition?*

Convincing clients to move on or transition to someone new can be difficult both for both parties. However, such a change will likely make you both happier in the end. As you open up spaces previously taken by clients who weren't ideal, you'll create space for those who do fit you better, creating a more positive outcome for everyone.

Budget

Once you've determined what you love to do, the way you provide it differently, who you ideally want to work with and what you want to accomplish by doing so, you'll have come quite a long way in establishing a course for success. To keep the momentum going, it's important to put these basic elements together with the different marketing techniques and strategies into a plan of action. In addition to defining the basics we've already outlined – are using tools that are a good fit for your vision and business - it's important to determine the time and money you can afford to put these strategies into action.

Now you may be thinking, "Money? Budget? The title of this book implies that I'm going to be learning FREE techniques. I'm confused!"

Let me clarify...

As I mentioned in the Foreword, I am a *Certified Guerrilla Marketing Coach* (CGMC). Guerilla marketing utilizes your time, energy, imagination, and current resources rather than

> "A bank is a place that will lend you money if you can prove that you don't need it."
>
> **Bob Hope**

expensive advertising to promote yourself. That's why I wrote this book and teach classes on free and easy ways to promote yourself. I definitely don't think it is necessary to drain your bank account to grow your business. After all, just because something costs a lot does not mean it's better.

But in terms of free marketing, we have to ask the question...

"Is anything really free?"

I've thought about this a lot and realized although there is an investment of some kind in most marketing, there are a few things

31

we can do that are absolutely free.

A few examples come to mind

- Smiling, that's one of your greatest marketing tools!

- Exhibiting a positive, enthusiastic attitude

- Being happy when your clients come in

- Showing confidence when meeting new people

- Using kind words instead of mean or derogatory ones

- Being polite, honest and friendly

- Living passionately

- Being prompt and professional

- Creating and holding an intention

- Actively listening to whomever is speaking to you

- What else can you add?

But other than the above, most marketing tools and strategies aren't completely free. Even if they don't cost you any cash, you will have to invest some of your other limited resources such as time or energy. Thus, while the title of the book is on target as much of what is shared in the following chapters is "free" to low cost – as well as "easy" - it's also important to become aware of, budget for and keep track of ALL the investments you are making in your business.

Start by giving some thought to how much time, money and energy you're willing to commit to growing your business each day, week and month. In general as you're growing a full-time practice, you may not have a large budget of cash and will instead spend more sweat equity to grow your business – at least in the beginning. You may also have some up-front cash investments along the way to purchase business cards, join networking groups or do mailings.

> "Invest three percent of your income in yourself (self-development) in order to guarantee your future."
>
> **Brian Tracy**

I suggest you use a typical work schedule of 30 – 40 hours a week as a basis for the time you commit to marketing and growing your business. As you start to fill in a few hours here and there with clients, the amount of hours marketing will likely drop back. If you continue to treat the marketing and business development part of your practice as seriously as you would a full schedule of clients, you'll fill up the bulk of your hours with appointments in no time.

If you're already in practice and are primarily looking to maintain your existing clientele while continuing to bring in a regular stream of new clients, it will likely make more sense to plan a block or two of regular business development time each week. You may also find you are investing more money than time (via discounts or incentives given in referral programs, birthday offers or marketing tools such as Constant Contact) than newer businesses. (See *Resources & Special Offers* at the back of the book for a free trial of Constant Contact). This happens because your schedule is getting more full with clients and so the supply of "extra" money on hand may become greater than supply of "extra" time.

To get started on your budget, make a list of all the actions you are currently taking each week or month to grow your business. Note the time they take and the money they cost to use. As you find additional tools or strategies that you want to try, come back to this list and add them to adjust your budget and see what you can afford.

Initial Marketing Budget

Marketing Tool or Activity	Cost	Time

Totals _____

How much time or money are you able to commit each week or month to help you achieve your business or marketing goals?

_____
_____
_____
_____

Tracking

No matter what types of marketing you invest in, you need to find out what works and what doesn't by tracking them all. If you aren't keeping track, how will you know for sure whether any particular promotion or tool is worth the investment you put into it?

Whether you use a spreadsheet, point of sale system or legal pad doesn't really matter. Keep a tally of all your marketing efforts and the results that come from them. (Download our *free* online resources including a Marketing Tracking Form at www.EveryTouchMarketing.com. Use the code **VOLUME1** when you check out ☺)

> "Don't measure yourself by what you have accomplished, but by what you should have accomplished with your ability."
>
> **John Wooden**

Once you know that something works to bring you business, do more of it. For example, a few years ago my summer packages were more popular than any promotion I'd ever done as a solo massage therapist. Knowing this, I extended the special sale for month after the planned end of the promo for even more sales. As a result I also decided to add multi-session packages to my offerings all year long!

Creating an Initial Marketing Plan

After getting clear on these key areas, you should have at least a rough idea of what you are trying to accomplish, who you are trying to reach through your marketing. Take a moment to summarize these areas here.

Passion/What I Love to Do Most

_____

_____

My Brand/Special Offering/What I Am Known For

_____

_____

My Goal(s)

_____

_____

My Audience

_____

_____

My Budget

_____

_____

My Best Tools and Marketing Actions

_____

_____

NOTES:

_____

_____

_____

_____

Initial Timeline and Actions

Week 1 _____

Week 2 _____

Week 3 _____

Week 4 _____

Week 5 _____

Week 6 _____

Week 7 _____

Week 8 _____

Week 9 _____

Week 10_____

Week 11_____

Week 12_____

Use this plan as a lens through which you plan all your marketing.

2 ATTRACTING NEW CLIENTS

If I've heard it once, I've heard it a thousand times from all kinds of personal service providers and businesses:

"I need more new clients."

Their work is good, their office or business location is appealing, but their schedules and wallets are not full. They are *discouraged, dissatisfied and stressed* about how to get where they want to be. Yet when I ask them what they are doing to reach out to new clients and prospects on a regular basis, they are often at a loss for words.

Why? There are many answers. Perhaps they weren't thoroughly trained in school in how to market themselves or their business. Maybe they weren't told that marketing and growing a business is a process, not a one-time event. And often, they

> "A satisfied customer is the best business strategy of all."
>
> **Michael LeBoeuf**

mistakenly think that the key to getting new clients is as simple, limited or expensive as placing an ad or two in their local newspaper or phone book. But the calls don't come. They feel worse and worse about themselves, their finances and their future.

The truth is that in a personal service industry – whether massage, skin care, chiropractic or personal training – traditional advertising is generally *not* the best way to find or get new clients. Instead, service providers have to look for ways to promote what they do that build credibility, encourage trust and empower some level of connection between them and their potential customers. These promotions are something that must become a part of each professional's work routine and schedule just like taking continuing education classes. In fact, as long as you are in business or practice, you must continue to reach out to new clients again and again.

39

As you go through the different ideas shared in this chapter, remember that some will fit you better than others. Use the techniques that best suit your strengths, personality, ideal clients and business as well as the goals you set in the last chapter.

Whatever techniques you choose to do, keep up the use of them consistently for a few months to see how effective they are in attracting new clients to your business. Most likely you will find a few strategies you like the best and decide to work with the most. But try give a variety of ideas a chance by testing a few at a time until you see what is the most effective and enjoyable for you.

Strategy #1 - Marketing People You Know (PYK)

When you are trying to get more clients and dollars into your practice or business, one of the most valuable assets you can utilize is the pool of people you already know – and who already know you. This group is made up your friends, family, social acquaintances, classmates, past work colleagues. It includes people you already socialize with at school, church and other groups as well as those you do business with. Since these people are already connected to you, they will normally be more supportive of you and your business than total strangers will be.

> "One of the challenges in networking is everybody thinks it's making cold calls to strangers. Actually, it's the people who already have strong trust relationships with you, who know you're dedicated, smart, a team player, who can help you."
>
> **Reid Hoffman**

It is important to let your PYKs know about your business and services while giving them a direct invitation (or several) along with a reason or two to try you out.

Begin by sending an announcement to everyone on your PYK list explaining what you offer – and the related benefits - along with an invitation and incentive to try your services out. This incentive could be a complimentary consultation, a free upgrade, or special pricing for new clients. I call this powerful yet easy combination…

Inform ~ Invite ~ Incent

The goal is to get your PYKS to try your services the first time, especially those who are potential ideal clients or can be a strong referral source for other future ideal clients. Try it – it works!

Whether you have a brand new business or just want to get the word out about what you do, begin by compiling a contact list or database of your PYKs who may become your future clients. Be sure to think about who in your list of PYKs could potentially introduce you to those who can benefit from your services or who have clients/customers who would also be interested in what you do.

For example, those who provide pain relief or wellness services may want to reach physicians and other medical providers. Those who work with athletes may want to connect with local gyms, yoga studios, activity clubs, or even support groups related to weight-loss.

People I Know Database

First Name	Last Name	Address	City	State	Zip	Email
Jennifer	Aniston	123 Hollywood Lane	Malibu	CA	01223	Jennifer@stars.com
George	Clooney	456 Good Looking Rd	LA	CA	01234	George@single.com
Kate	Hudson	789 Blondie Blvd	San Jose	CA	05678	Kate@blonde.com
Ryan	Gosling	1 Cool and Crazy St	Malibu	CA	01223	Ryan@surfsup.com

Once you have compiled your database, formulate a plan for sharing your business details, services and benefits, as well as special opportunities such as discounts or other incentives that will appeal to them as clients or referral sources. Keep these folks in the loop as you hire new staff, add services, and host events. Of course, if you are staying in touch with them via email, be sure make it easy for them to opt out or to adjust what notifications they get from you.

As the lines between beauty, wellness and health continue to merge, finding ways to connect and cross promote with these folks is vital to your business' well-being.

Other PYK Ideas

- Visit your bank, accountant, florist or any you do business with regularly, taking with you some coupons for your business. Tell them you wanted to say thank you for all they do for you and that you'd love to see them and their staff members sometime. You'll create goodwill and buzz through showing your appreciation for them.

- Take time to follow up with people who have previously expressed interest in doing business with you, cross-promoting one another, or even in buying a gift certificate. Let them know you have an open appointment, a special, or an idea for working together even if the last time you followed up they weren't ready to move forward.

- Go through past emails, old phone messages and retired appointment books to rediscover people you haven't seen in awhile and need to reconnect with. You may be surprised at the hidden opportunities that you can now collect on.

- Revisit relationships with current colleagues and companies you've previously partnered with to see how you can be of service to each other now. Think about ways to work together to generate new business or excitement around both your businesses and see what you can dream up.

- Always be looking for the opportunity in how you can create win-win situations with current vendors, clients and colleagues beyond today's service, meeting or event. Often there are new and profitable cross-promotions and marketing opportunities in the relationships you already have.

Strategy #2 - Networking
(or Getting to Know People You Don't Know Yet)

Networking for business is simply about making professional connections that can be of help to you and others down the road. You never know what solutions or opportunities may come just by meeting one or two new people. I encourage all professionals and business owners to be prepared to share their business with others and to be open to the possibilities that come from "planting" and "watering" the seeds of networking.

Successful people are often involved in a variety of groups from their church or children's schools to neighborhood associations and/or the boards and committees that make up a variety or political, civic and charitable organizations. These are all good places

> "Networking is an essential part of building wealth."
>
> **Armstrong Williams**

for networking and getting to know people in your community and establish more meaningful personal or business relationships with people you know in these groups. It also allows you to quietly "sell" yourself without being "salesy" about it. If you go to networking events and meetings with the idea that you are going to establish or enhance personal relationships with others rather than "making a sale," you'll have a much better chance of long-term success.

One of the common complaints I've heard about networking is from folks who aren't comfortable meeting new people or being in big group settings. In fact, I was one of these people many years ago when I first became a massage therapist. But as necessity mandated I meet new people to build my practice, I quickly learned to look at a room full of strangers as a room full of potential clients. It became much easier to talk to people I didn't yet know about everything – and especially my business - after that attitude adjustment.

To grow your business more quickly, I suggest you get started by visiting a variety of networking or "leads" groups. Some of these such as *Business Network International* (BNI) or the *eWomen Network* are mainly focused on networking. Others, such as your local *Chamber of Commerce* or other local Merchants' Association are organizations built to help companies succeed and offer a variety of programs beyond networking groups. Most networking groups have regularly scheduled events of various sizes and formats that are perfect opportunities to connect with other business owners and professionals.

> "No employer today is independent of those about him. He cannot succeed alone, no matter how great his ability or capital. Business today is more than ever a question of cooperation."
>
> **Orison Swett Marden**

Additionally, organizations such as the *Chamber* usually provide a huge array of benefits for a fairly small investment. This can include benefits such as inclusion in a member directory; business web site links and/or profiles on the organization's web site; leadership training and development; sponsorship opportunities for community events; discounts for products and services from other members; and more. These organizations can also there to help you prosper through educational and promotional opportunities.

Whatever groups you seek out, go to a few meetings as a guest to see what the group is like and if they are accepting members in your profession. See where you feel most comfortable and what type of group best suits your schedule, business and budget. Prices for membership in networking organizations generally vary from being completely free to costing several hundred dollars a year.

*****

Another idea for networking is to make friends with your so called

45

"competitors" by creating a trade-oriented networking group in your area. Whether you decide to host a group for similar professionals, complimentary businesses or just people who are interested in health, fitness, beauty or wellness, being in charge of a group like this can bring you added credibility, exposure and tons of useful contacts. (One organization that helps create and equip new and independent networking groups is *MeetUp.com*.)

When you get together with your trade group, focus on learning and sharing how each business or person works, what they specialize in and who their ideal clients are. Rather than being in competition for the exact same folks, you'll more than likely find people that are resources for clients you cannot help or squeeze into your schedule. And you'll often find the camaraderie in trade groups very rewarding.

By getting to know each other, you'll find allies that can help you when equipment breaks, staffing situations arise or even product suppliers let you down. You'll also gain some of the most valuable referrals you can get – those from respected and trusted colleagues –

> "Honor bespeaks worth. Confidence begets trust. Service brings satisfaction. Cooperation proves the quality of leadership."
>
> **James Cash Penney**

and some good friends who know what you go through as an owner. You may also find opportunities to partner with one another to cross-promote, share advertising, host events and more. Networking and working cooperatively can make all of your businesses stronger and more resilient in an ever-changing world.

HOW to Network Effectively

Unfortunately, too many people misunderstand the value of networking or erroneously believe that "networking" simply means showing up at a gathering and passing out a few business cards. Truly effective networking actually IS work but can also have tremendous payoffs. To make your networking experiences more beneficial, you'll need to do some preparation and planning for steps to take in advance of the event, at the event, and following the event.

Before the networking event:

As you prepare for each networking event, do a little research. Who does this event draw? (Men/Women, Biz Owners, Job Seekers, etc). Who are the event organizers? (Chamber, Church, Activities Club). What are some possible problems this group has that you can solve? (Stress, sun damage, aging concerns) Now you can begin to brainstorm on ideas of what to talk about when you meet people!

Also, be sure to determine what it is you want to accomplish or get by going to an event. Do you want to meet five new people and collect their business cards? Is it to introduce your corporate

> "Before anything else, preparation is the key to success."
>
> **Alexander Graham Bell**

services to ten new companies? Perhaps you want to meet the person in charge of the event to discuss sponsoring the next one? Or introduce this season's new, hot service? Whatever your intent, your goals should determine your planned actions. Be specific and make a plan to reach your goal.

Once you decide what to promote, create a short statement or "elevator speech" to explain your service. Do it in a way that intrigues others without using jargon. Example: Instead of "I'm an esthetician" try "I help people of all ages look their best." Instead of saying "I specialize in Myofacial Release" say "I help people get out of pain." If they're interested, they'll ask how, and you can share your offer.

Along with your elevator speech, be ready to share some kind of an offer to get people take action. For example, if you want to attract new facial clients, you might have "20% off your first facial when you schedule by _____ " printed on the back of your card. Fill in a reasonable expiration date and then share the cards and offer with each person you talk to at the event.

Whether it's a free consultation or a new client special, have an offer or promotion that fits the needs of (ideal) clients you're targeting. Example: Group - Young professional women; Need: Looking their best/stress reduction; Offer: free make-up lesson with any service booked in August.

At the event:

> "Work hard, stay positive, and get up early. It's the best part of the day."
>
> **George Allen, Sr.**

Arrive early or at the time the event begins. Contrary to the theory that it is fashionable to be late, you'll actually make better contacts and have more quality time with people if you are prompt. This is because when there are fewer people milling about, you are more likely to have a conversation that gets beyond "Hi, my name is. . ."

If there is someone specific you want to meet at an event that is supposed to attend, keep your eye on the entryway for their arrival. If you don't see them, every thirty minutes or so, go back to the registration desk and see who else has signed in. If you don't know who they are, ask the registrar if they can point the person out.

Don't be one of those "hit and run" networkers. When talking with people be sure to use their name and ask about their work or company as most people love to talk about themselves. Concentrate on the person you are speaking with and show a genuine interest in their story. Spend at least five minutes talking with them, introduce them to others when appropriate, and always thank them for their time when you part.

Also, look at each person you meet as a potential client or referral source. See how that idea changes the way you speak to them, the things you discuss or the courtesy you show them. Look for opportunities to help them in their endeavors and to let them know what you do. And of course, even when networking in this casual way, make sure you've got business cards to share with them.

After the event:

If appropriate, take action to contact the people you met — or wanted to meet but didn't - after the event. Put them on follow up email list or call them a day or two later to touch base on something you had previously spoken about. For instance, if at the event they said "I've been thinking of

> "Action is the foundational key to all success."
>
> **Pablo Picasso**

getting a massage. . ." call them and say, "After we spoke I had a few cancellations. Would you like to schedule a massage next week?" Or if you had discussed a product, class or other information that could be of help to them, follow up with relevant details.

If you prefer using social media networks, you may be able get in touch through your preferred site and send a private message or request to connect. To do this through LinkedIn or Facebook, you can do a quick search by their name or company and then send them an invitation to connect or become friends. If you prefer Twitter, you can follow them and connect through direct messages. Whichever site or app you choose to connect on, I suggest that you include a reminder of how and where you met.

Networking Follow-up Template:

Use this as a guide only. Try to inject your own personality and the tone of your meeting or conversation with the person. If you only met them briefly, the note would probably need to be more formal. If you really felt a good rapport, you can be more casual.

What is most important with this follow up and any "marketing tool" is to include a call to action (ask them to call for an appointment, email you, check out your web site, etc.) Also be sure they know how to reach you again so include your card and/or make sure your contact info is in the body of the email or your email signature.

Use the template below as a guide to your own networking follow-up notes. You can use the same template as a guideline or script for follow-up calls as well!

Dear _____ -

It was so nice to meet you at (name of event) (last night, last week, last month, etc). I really enjoyed (talking with you, hearing about your company, your joke about the elephant, etc.) and will share your name with my clients who are looking for (aluminum siding, a new accountant, a good psychiatrist, etc).

I also wanted to send you a copy of our service menu so you are aware of all the services we offer. We can schedule for the (massage, make-up consultation, bikini wax, etc.) that we discussed whenever you are ready. Just call or email to set up your appointment.

I look forward to seeing you soon.

Sincerely /Yours Truly -

Your signature

If you are sending an email follow up, you can attach a PDF copy of a menu or share a link to your website. Of course, when using traditional mail, always enclose your business card and/or a service menu or brochure with your note. (I actually like to put some type of inspiring card like the one below that I created for my coaching business.)

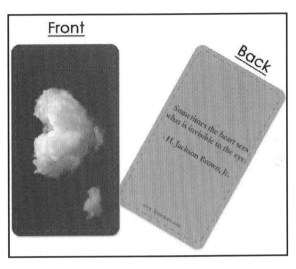

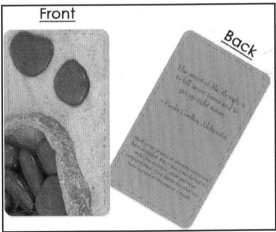

More Tips for Success in Networking

- Take PLENTY of business cards to every networking meeting as well as a pen. When you get a business card from someone else, write a note on the back about your conversation, common interests or how you plan to follow up with them. This is incredibly helpful when it is time to add them to a database or address book – and for following up with them at a future time.

- Take a pocket notebook with you to networking events. As you talk to people, make notes in your notebook about the ideas that came up or what promises you made to each person to follow up.

- Think of everyone you meet as a potential client or referral source. Doing so will help you become a magnet for new business and opportunities. Ask people how you can help them and their business rather than just promoting yourself. Then do what you can to help them. You might be surprised at how this builds loyalty, business and referrals.

- Think of ways to educate prospects and clients about what you do, why you do and the benefits so they will have a better understanding of how your services can help them and others.

- At each meeting, put on an approachable, confident look and attitude. Reach out to those who are alone seem or nervous. Ask about them, what they do, if they've been to this group before. Look for ways to help them and their business first. Then tell them what you do and share your offer and card.

- After each networking meeting, go through your cards or notes about who you need to follow up with - and then do it! Add them to your address book or database, send them referrals and start building a new PYK relationship. Don't forget – take this step!

- Try to find a networking group that you like and will go to regularly, if not every time they gather. The more the "regulars" see your face and get to know, like and trust you, the better your chances of getting business and referrals from them.

- Ask other people for help in marketing your business. Sometimes we feel like we have to go it alone when there are actually many related businesses and professionals who'd like nothing more than to see us succeed. Make a list of business that could be a good match for cross promotions. Then start reaching out to explore the possibilities.

- Don't burn bridges with clients, employees, employers or business acquaintances. You never know when that person could reappear in your life as a potential ally...or an enemy. True, not all relationships are salvageable, but do try to take the high road when making business transitions. It can pay unknown dividends in the long run.

- Whether you network in person or on the web through social media, approach these new relationships with the mindset of how you can be of help to others. This could mean referring them business, providing them with useful resources or even becoming a client of theirs. And as your relationship and rapport grows, they will be more likely to do business with you than when you first meet.

*****

The bottom line is that networking is good for your business. So be prepared for networking wherever you go. Think of every person you meet as someone who is looking for solutions to a problems - one perhaps you can help them solve. Turn them from an unknown stranger into a PYK. Continue to Inform, Invite and Incent them throughout your relations ship and before you know it, the appointments, sales and referrals will start to flow.

Strategy #3 - Ask For Referrals

So many people talk about the need for word-of-mouth advertising but don't know how to get it. Well, the reality is you have to start with your own word-of-mouth. To get referrals for your business, you need to ask for them, period. This is one of the best and most effective ways to build and grow your business as it provides new clients a much more personal and comfortable introduction to you and your business than any ad ever can.

Be willing to reward people with a thank you or referral fee to those who help you promote your business. Whether you thank them with a discount, free products and services or a gift certificate to their favorite shop,

> "In sales, a referral is the key to the door of resistance."
>
> **Bo Bennett**

many people will work harder for you when they know they will get something in return. *Note – depending on your discipline and location, referral programs or rewards may not be allowed. Check the laws in your state or province as well as any trade or professional associations for specific guidelines.*

If you are able to offer a reward for referrals, make your reward program *as simple as possible.* Some examples include offering a free product or discount toward their next purchase, a gift certificate to a local store or something else of your choosing. Whatever the reward, if you can't explain what you want the referring party to do in order to get the reward easily in a sentence or two, it's too hard.

Or if you have a Points' Club or Loyalty Program, you could also add a pre-determined amount of points to that person's account for each referral they send. Whatever the reward, it should be communicated or given to the client immediately following the referral.

Once you decide on a referral program or incentive that is easy to explain and affordable to maintain, make sure to tell your clients about it. Train yourself (and your staff) to tell every one of your good clients how much you appreciate their business and would like to have more clients just like them. Ask for their help in growing more successful by referring their friends and family, neighbors, co-workers to you.

If you work for someone else, talk to the business owner or manager about any special ideas or rewards they currently (or are planning to) offer for referrals. Of course, follow up on each referral to get the new client scheduled. Be sure to thank the person who gave the referral promptly and keep on asking!

Sample Scripts for Asking for Referrals:

 # 1 – Brief

You: "For every new body wrap client you send in, you'll receive a $10 certificate good towards any regularly priced retail product or service at Spa Ti Dah."

#2 – Extended

You: "Thanks for coming in today, Rachel. It was great to see you. Before you leave, I want to tell you about the new referral program Spa Ti Da is offering. If you've enjoyed my services here and know anyone that might benefit from them, I'd really appreciate your referral."

Client: "You know I love coming here and would be glad to help you grow your business."

You: "That's awesome. For every new client you send in, you'll receive _____ *(example: a certificate for $10 off your next service, a free product, etc.) that you can use or give to someone else. Also, here are a few of my cards/our new client invitations for you to pass along to your friends and family. And be sure they give us your name when they come in."*

Client: "Oh that's great. I have a few friends I plan to tell about you."

You: "Wonderful. I really appreciate your support! Have a wonderful weekend!"

Client: "Thanks! You too."

*****

Use Referral Cards

Maybe you've asked for referrals in the past and have gotten quite a few or not as many as you would have liked. Take your referral promotions a step further by printing business card or gift certificate sized referral cards to share with your clients. Then make it a win/win by providing an incentive for the new client coming in as well as a reward for the client who referred them.

Make the referral process easy for all parties by adding a blank or space where the referring client can write their name or company name. And if you work in a place with more than one practitioner, make sure new clients know to ask for you specifically. Give out at least two or three business cards or new client passes to give to prospects.

How to use new client referral cards and certificates:

- Give at least three to every client you see
- Give with/in place of your business card at networking event
- Pass out anywhere you interact with a sales person or cashier
- Send them out in your Christmas/holiday cards
- Include them with retail or gift certificate purchases
- Hand them out with appointment reminder cards
- Give them to clients to send out in their holiday cards
- Send them to businesses you patronize to put in employee paychecks or pass out to their clients

- Ask other small businesses to put a stack at their cash register or wherever they post info from other businesses
- Leave as an additional tip when you eat out
- Enclose in birthday cards to your friends

See below for an example of one referral certificate I've used:

Gift Certificates: Front side

New Client Certificate

Spalutions - Massage Therapy Office of Felicia Brown, LMBT
523 State Street · Greensboro, NC 27405 · 336.508.0790

To

Value

Referred by

Authorized Signature   Expires on

Gift Certificates: Back side

Valid for New Clients Only
Certificate good towards 60 or 90 minute massage sessions with Felicia

Hours by Appointment ~ 24 Hour Cancellation Requested
Call 336.508.0790 now to schedule your appointment!

Are you ready for an $8000 idea?

In the section *Your Ideal Clients* in Chapter 1, I talked about one of the most successful promotions I've ever had which involved referrals. Rather than being aimed at large groups of random people like a promotion on sites like Groupon or Living Social would be, this campaign was very specifically aimed at new *ideal clients* that were friends, colleagues or family members of my current ideal clients.

I had one hundred gift certificates (see the next page) printed up for Complimentary 30 Minute Massages with the intention to give two to each of my regular clients and to mail the others to former or inactive clients that I wanted to see again.

Next I created a flyer (see the page after the gift certificate) that I sent in an email telling my clients about the promotion. I also had it posted in my office at my reception desk next to a stack of printed copies of it.

As each regular client came in for their regular massage during the time of the promotion, I handed them a flyer along with their two certificates and explained the promotion. I told them that the free certificates were only to go to people who met the qualifications on the flyer.

Most people said something along the lines of "Wow. I'll really have to think about that!"

My response: "Exactly!"

The whole point was to specifically target *my ideal clients*, not to give a free massage to every grocery store clerk and mailman in my neighborhood. (No offense to any of these individuals or professions. If I had the time, money and desire to give free massages away to everyone who wanted them, then there would be no need for me to have defined my ideal clients or targeted this promotion!)

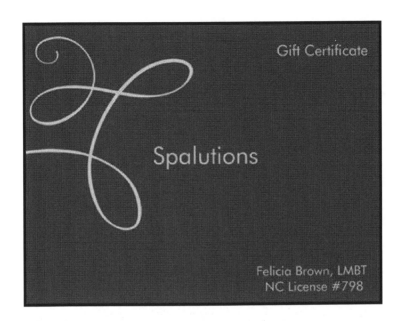

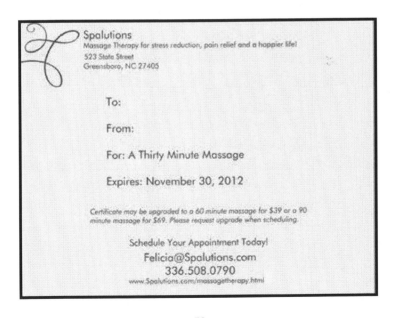

Spalutions
Massage Therapy for stress reduction, pain relief and a happier life!
523 State Street
Greensboro, NC 27405

To:

From:

For: A Thirty Minute Massage

Expires: November 30, 2012

Certificate may be upgraded to a 60 minute massage for $39 or a 90 minute massage for $69. Please request upgrade when scheduling.

Schedule Your Appointment Today!
Felicia@Spalutions.com
336.508.0790
www.Spalutions.com/massagetherapy.html

Give the Gift of Massage FOR FREE!

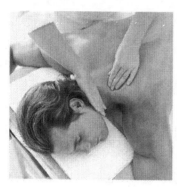

I'm providing each of my clients the opportunity to give the gift of massage to a friend or family member at no cost to you.

Through September 30th, I'm offering up to two (2) thirty minute massage gift certificates* to each of my clients to give away.

Specifically these certificates are for people who will be a good fit for my business, style of massage, pricing and personality.

My request is you give these certificates to people who:

- *Are nice, friendly, interesting people who value massage therapy as a healing art and valid part of their wellness program*
- *Have schedules that allow them to have massage appointments between the hours of 10 AM and 5 PM Monday thru Friday (or the occasional Saturday)*
- *Are looking for a regular massage therapist or want to receive massage at least once a month*
- *Have not seen me before or in the last 2 years*
- *Preferably live or work within 5 miles of my office*

New clients receiving the certificates may upgrade them to longer sessions of 60 or 90 minutes by paying an additional fee or $39 or $69 respectively. Or if you'd prefer to upgrade the session before giving someone the certificate, you may pay for the upgrade when you get their certificate.

(*Certificates must be redeemed by November 30, 2012.)

New Client Program
Pre- book your next session and save $10

Or extend the savings!

Enjoy Life Now*

Package just $210

Enjoy three
One Hour Massages for $70 *each*
- a $30 savings!

Freedom from Pain & Stress*
Package for just $390

Free yourself from pain and stress with
Six One Hour Massages
at the incredible price of just $65 each!
You save $90☺

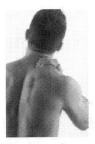

* Thirty minute packages also available

Packages are for new clients only, are non-transferable and may not be shared. Special packages rates are valid through June 30, 2013. Not valid with any other discounts, specials or offers. Prices not valid for individual sessions – package must be paid in-full to receive special pricing. Services provided by Felicia Brown, LMBT (NC License #798) unless otherwise noted. Thanks for your referrals and business!

Felicia Brown, LMBT – 523 State Street ~ Greensboro, NC 27405
Call 336.508.0790 or email Felicia@Spalutions.com for details or to
schedule your next appointment.

When the new clients came in, I asked good questions, listened intently to the answers, and paid attention any cues they gave about wanting or needing to relax, manage stress, or simply get massage. I also gave them information about how to save money or get a better value on their future appointments with me via the flyer on the last page. I also implemented one or more of my various rebooking strategies (see the next section on *Getting Clients to Return through Rebooking*)

So what were the results???

First the cost: The initial amount of cash invested in printing the certificates and postage for mailing certificates to a few former clients I hoped to reactivate was a whopping total of **$72.39.**

I also spent about thirty minutes designing the **Give the Gift of Massage For Free** flyer. This also included the time to create in two or three emails that were sent to existing clients. I spent another thirty minutes on the **New Client Program** flyer I used to encourage the new clients who came in to reschedule another massage or purchase a multi-session package. I printed these myself so there was not much of a cost associated with them.

If I value the hour of production time at $80, what I charge for a massage, my total investment in this promotion was $392.39. But if I count my cash investment only, the total spent was **just $72.39.**

Next, the clients: From this promotion, over a period of eight months, my practice gained twenty new clients and revived two formerly regular clients, many of whom have become regulars who receive services weekly or monthly. Out of the new clients, only twelve actually used a free 30 minute massage certificate. The rest were referred by the other new clients. The twelve "free massage" certificates redeemed in this initial promotion resulted in me giving away only six (6) hours of my massage time, valued at **$240.**

Finally, the revenue. Over approximately eight months, this targeted promotion generated **$8431.82** (including all tips paid to me) in my massage therapy practice. And it's still making money. After direct expenses, this promotion brought in *over twenty times* what I invested in it in just over eight months. Since I many of these clients have continued to be on-going regulars – and have continued to refer their friends and family – I expect this number to more than double each year in the future. That's what I call a successful promotion!!

Here's how it broke down over the first 8 months...

Individual Services and Packages:	$6635.87
Retail Purchases:	$1198.95
Tips:	$597.00
Gross Revenue from Promotion:	**$8431.82**
Less Total Invested:	$392.39
Net Revenue from Promotion:	**$8039.43**

While these numbers may seem out of reach if you are still getting clear on your goals and exactly who your ideal clients are, I have no doubt you can get the same kind of results through this kind of promotion with the right amount of planning and preparation. Just take the time to target it properly and be diligent about implementing all the steps along the way.

Whatever promotion you use, don't be afraid to ask for referrals! If you do a good job and clients like you, they'll want to help you succeed. Pay it forward by referring business to others when you can.

Strategy #4 - Get the Word Out with Press Releases

Take advantage of the many free marketing opportunities available by blowing your own horn. Though in and of themselves, press releases and the media opportunities that come from them don't always lead new clients to your front door directly, they can help provide you with a higher level of credibility, professional reputation and buzz that make a prospective client's decision to try you out a bit easier.

Send out press releases to your local newspapers, business publications, and area magazines about *anything* newsworthy that you have done recently, but especially in relation to your business or practice. This can include things like continuing education completed, appointments to committees and boards, and special events you have planned, such as open houses or health fairs. You can also often send press releases to professional journals and magazines, although the content will probably need to be revised so it is more relevant to your colleagues rather than consumers.

> "Publicity, publicity, publicity is the greatest moral factor and force in our public life."
>
> **Joseph Pulitzer**

Not sure where to get started? Begin by brainstorming about how your company might be interesting to the media. What causes do you support or events do you host? Are you involved in professional activities on state, national or international level? Do you or any of your staff members have a unique background or story that people would be interested in? Just start looking around for opportunities for promotion and begin getting the word out.

Most newspapers and business publications will have some kind of "Who's Who" or "People and Places" section for small announcements such as new hires, trainings and certifications, etc. More in-depth or interesting stories, such as a large expansion or your work with a particular charity may be of interest to the local or business sections of a publication. Whatever the case, make yourself familiar with how each media outlet you plan to contact is set up so that you can request proper placement of your information. It is important as well to find out about deadlines for dated information so that you can get everything in on time.

Whatever you send in should be concisely written and should include your email address, business address and phone number in case someone from the publication or other news outlet needs to contact you. Also

> "Publicity can be terrible. But only if you don't have any."
>
> **Jane Russell**

include links or web addresses for your website and any social media profiles. Any, all or none of this may also be listed with your write-up, but be sure it is complete and accurate just in case.

Before you send out anything, remember to proofread your work for grammar and spelling errors, as well as clarity. It is a real waste of time and energy to send out the wrong information! If needed, have a friend or colleague read what you have written if you are not sure how it sounds or think something might be missing.

Whenever possible use email to send out press releases along with a recent digital head shot photo and other related company information such as a press kit, service menu or professional bio. If you have to use snail mail, it is still a good idea to include your head-shot or any relevant photos with your name and business name written on the back, and your business card or brochure. Make the most of that stamp!

Once your press release or article is printed (or you get some actual TV), post it where your clients can read it including linking it on your website and social media profiles. They may not have seen it but will surely want to. If your media mention looks especially impressive, you may want to think about having it framed and hung in your office or displayed at your reception desk. You'd be surprised how impressed people are by that sort of thing!

After your press release or article comes out, send a thank you note to the reporter or columnist who worked with you. Including a coupon or gift certificate for a discounted or free session or just a small token gift is another way to create good will. These small touches will stand out in the writer or reporter's mind and prompt them to call you for future needs.

Press release checklist:

Ready to get to work on informing the media and the public about just how interesting you are? Make sure your press release answers the following questions, includes a quote from you about the accomplishment or event you are discussing, and is informational only (no selling.) Think about the audience that reads, watches or listens to this media outlet and what topics are of interest to them.

- ✓ TITLE – This should be eye catching and pique the reader's interest.

- ✓ WHO – This includes you and any other key people or staff members mentioned in the press release as well as the identity of your business and/or other organizations that are a focus of the press release.

- ✓ WHAT – What happened or will be happening that is of interest to the reader?

- ✓ WHERE - In what location did or will this item of interest take place?

- ✓ WHEN – Last week, last month, next week, next month, etc. Remember timeliness is important before and after events.

- ✓ WHY – What was the cause, purpose, reason behind the event, training, award?

- ✓ HOW – What brought this about? What did it take?

- ✓ PHOTOS – Digital photos of you (a high resolution professional head shot is best), your business and any other key scenes or people related to the article.

- ✓ RELATED DETAILS, CONTACT INFO, KEY WORDS – Make the job of the reporter/writer(s) as easy as possible by including pertinent information that can be of use in crafting an article or story without a lot of research on their part.

- ✓ A QUOTE FROM YOU ABOUT THE EVENT – Include information that explains more about why the event is meaningful to you, helpful to others, worth attending, etc.

Sample Press Release

FOR IMMEDIATE RELEASE

AMTA Member Selected as 2009 Spa Person of the Year

Greensboro, NC – May 5, 2009 – Felicia Brown, owner of *Spalutions!* and an AMTA member, has been selected as the 2009 Spa Person of the Year. This award is given each year by the Day Spa Association. Brown was honored at the 2009 Day Spa Expo in Las Vegas, NV.

"It is an incredible honor to be chosen as the Spa Person of the Year." said Brown. " My career in the massage and spa industries has given me the opportunity to work with many individuals who are just as deserving of this award. I am grateful to Hannelore Leavy and the Day Spa Association for selecting me. Like the DSA, I am committed to supporting and enriching the spa industry."

Brown has won numerous awards for her business skills and accomplishments including **Top Entrepreneurs of 2009** and **Top 25 Movers & Shakers of 2008** by *Business Leader Magazine*. Other awards include **2007 Volunteer of the Year** (American Massage Therapy Association) **2005 Small Business Person of the Year** (Greensboro Chamber of Commerce), **2004 Women in Business** (*The Business Journal*), and **2003 Forty Leaders Under Forty** (*The Business Journal*).

About Felicia Brown

Felicia Brown, LMBT is the owner of *Spalutions*, (www.Spalutions.com) a firm that provides business and marketing coaching for massage, spa and wellness professionals. She has written for and been featured or quoted in numerous trade publications including *DAYSPA, Spa Magazine, Skin Inc., Massage Therapy Journal, Massage Magazine, Massage & Bodywork, Spa Management Journal* and *Dermascope*.

About The Day Spa Association

The Day Spa Association (DSA) is a professional membership-based trade organization founded whose focus is to serve as the primary business resource for day spa professionals through educational seminars and workshops, research studies, and publications

Related links:
Spalutions: http://www.spalutions.com
Day Spa Association: www.dayspassociation.com
Keywords: Felicia Brown, Spalutions, Day Spa Association
Contact Information:
Spalutions ~ 523 State Street
Greensboro, NC 27405
336.508.0790 Direct
Felicia@Spalutions.com

Your Turn☺ - Press Release Outline

TITLE:

WHO:

WHAT:

WHERE:

WHEN:

WHY:

HOW:

QUOTE:

RELATED DETAILS, CONTACT INFO, KEY WORDS:

PHOTO:

Draft press release:

_____

_____

_____

_____

_____

_____

_____

_____

Remember you can send out press releases as often as you like. Local news media are there to report what is going on in your community so use them. The time and energy spent on getting this free publicity will be well worth the visibility, credibility and goodwill brought to you, your business, and your profits!

Strategy #5 - Look and Ask for Publicity

A few years ago, I got an email from the **National Certification Board for Therapeutic Massage and Bodywork.** It asked if I knew anyone who should be featured in an upcoming newsletter. They were looking for a member who had done something noteworthy and that other members would be interested in reading about. I wrote them back and told them I thought they should write about me, listing a few of my accomplishments and qualifications. (Nationally certified since 1994, massage therapist turned spa owner turned spa consultant, Small Business Person of the Year in 2005, and so on.) They agreed. The email newsletter with the article about me went out to everyone on their mailing list.

There was also an unexpected bonus. After I was interviewed for the online newsletter, I got a call back asking if I could do an additional interview for the print version which was mailed to about 100,000 people and schools. Of course I said yes and so just a couple of months later, I got another plug in the newsletter.

> "Whoever controls the media, controls the mind."
>
> **Jim Morrison**

Another example: many years ago I self-published a newsletter about business and marketing for massage therapists. While my paid subscription list was never very big, I was able to use the newsletter to open the door to write for other publications. I sent copies of it to all the massage trade publications I knew of at the time (**MTJ**, **Massage Magazine** and **Massage**) with a letter mentioning that I would like to write for them. In turn, each publication asked me to write one or more articles for them. I did which created a much bigger name, reputation and resume for me in the massage and spa industries. I also shared these articles with my clients and students which continued to grow my reputation as an expert in the field.

70

What can you write about to get your name in local or trade publications?

_____

_____

Other publicity comes from knowing the right people. For example, a good friend of mine used to work at an area television station - he was the weather man. When I had an event going on at my office, I asked him to help me get coverage of the event on his station. As a result, I made numerous appearances over the years on that station and as result became known as THE massage therapist (then later THE spa owner) in town.

Who do you know that can help you get on television or in the local newspaper?

_____

_____

Some of the best publicity I've gotten is from winning awards such as Best Local Spa, Women in Business). Even if you don't win, you can still get great press just for being nominated. But you could win so why not ask someone to nominate you or nominate yourself?! Either way, getting your name mentioned in conjunction with being nominated for or winning an award is something you can use to gain more publicity in your professional trade organizations, local publications and so on. Every award, article, mention or television appearance help you to gain better credibility and professional exposure – and more clients!

What local, national or trade awards might you be eligible to win?

_____

_____

If you are able to take advantage of unexpected media opportunities, interviews and appearances, get additional mileage out of them by sharing the articles or clips with your clients in your next newsletter, blog or e-blast. Not only will a whole new set of people will see them but your credibility will be strengthened even more.

If you are serious about getting PR for your business, consider adding a press kit to your marketing tools. Whether printed or online (both are advised) it should paint a picture of your business and answers the who, what, why, where, when and how questions and include images that you want to share with the media and public. Think logo, treatment rooms, actual treatments, etc.

Also, be ready when unexpected publicity or promotional opportunities arise. This means staying alert to media calls and inquiries, having a topic or two that you can speak about in front of a group on short notice, and following up on such opportunities pronto. That's how I've gotten most of the PR opportunities in my business and the same could happen for you. ☺

> "If Jesus were here today, he wouldn't be riding around on a donkey. He'd be taking a plane, he'd be using the media."
>
> **Joel Osteen**

Finally, be on the lookout for unexpected places to promote yourself such as online radio/TV shows. One I've appeared on regularly to promote my coaching business and classes is *The Massage Nerd Show* (*http://www.massagenerd.com.*) Look for similar shows that reach your ideal clients or create your own at BlogTalkRadio.com.

Other PR Ideas

- Collect and Share Testimonials. People like to see that their current or potential spa or service provider is well regarded and liked. Whenever someone gives a positive review, compliment or testimonial about your business or work, ask for their permission to use it as a part of your marketing. Then repeat the good news posting it on your website or including it in your client newsletter.

- Start collecting the thank you cards/emails, newspaper articles, and other upbeat comments made about your business, services or staff. Put them all together in a scrapbook or photo album to display in your waiting or relaxation area so that other guests can read them. This also provides an opportunity to prompt or ask other clients to contribute their own sentiments.

- Create a guestbook for your waiting room where clients can jot down their thoughts about their visit, session or experience at your office. It could be a journal or guest book like what many Bed &Breakfasts offer. Signing it is voluntary and since it is already visible, clients who write in it are giving their permission to share their words there just by writing them in the book. Make sharing the guestbook a part of your office or spa tour and invite everyone to contribute their favorite memory of their visit.

- Getting your name out there as an expert in your field can be done in lots of different ways. One way is to comment on other people's blogs, especially those that are read by your target audience. For example, other educators and consultants might weigh in on my blogs to broaden their audience and add their own twist to the advice I share. Where can you add your wisdom?

- If you haven't already done so, create a professional bio or byline of varying lengths to be used with articles you write or to be used to introduce you at classes or speaking engagements. These can also be posted on your website, blog or social media pages if appropriate and can come in handy more than you know.

- If you haven't already done so, create a professional bio or byline of varying lengths to be used with articles you write or to be used to introduce you at classes or speaking engagements. These can also be posted on your website, blog or social media pages if appropriate and can come in handy more than you know.

- Get noticed by doing some public speaking. Make a list of business/health/spa topics you feel comfortable speaking about. Look at local meetings/events calendars to find events or groups where your topics could be of interest.

- Find interesting ways to get PR. For example, on Facebook I was once a finalist in a contest held by a restaurant where I used to work. Just by posting on their fan page I reconnected with a couple of old friends and clients. Also by submitting an entry for their contest I won a $250 GC and was interviewed for the book that is being published on the eatery. PR is PR. Look for it!

- Be willing to go that extra mile to promote your business. Whether that means getting up at 5 am to do a live TV broadcast or stretching beyond your comfort zone to speak to a large group about the benefits of your services, being the go-to person about your field or in your area can get you added PR and exposure. Take a deep breath and grab ahold of these opportunities when they present themselves.

- Support students and future professionals of the salon and spa industry. Whether you take on an intern or offer information sessions or tours to up and coming graduates, go out of your way to befriend these people. They will come to you first when looking for a job and likely refer you to their own clients, colleagues, and friends while they are in school – or even after – all of which will improve your reputation and business.

- Become quotable by participating in trade and local magazine surveys, reader forums and blogs. If you participate often and have worthwhile things to say, your quote may be featured on the publication's website or even in their print magazine. This gives you as a professional a new feather in your cap and gives you the ability to state that you were quoted by that publication on your website, in your resume, bio and press kit.

- Share your media quotes with your followers and fans by posting a link or PDF copy of each mention on your website, blog, social media fan pages or profiles. Take this a step further by creating a media page on your website with direct links to each article and mention. Then publicize the news internally to your staff so they are aware of the publicity and understand your position/opinion – and can brag to their own clients.

Strategy #6 - Working Together is Better!

When considering partnering with other businesses and organizations, I look for people that have complimentary beliefs or work ethics to mine, have a similar type of ideal client base, or have qualities or achievements I just plain admire. The point of this for me is to get to know people that I will enjoy working with in some way or another and that I think will enjoy working with me. Life is too short for relationships, work or otherwise, that aren't pleasant or productive on some level. Here are a few ways you can work with the individuals and business you like and respect.

Cross-market with Other Wellness and Fitness Professionals

> "Unity is strength... when there is teamwork and collaboration, wonderful things can be achieved."
>
> **Mattie Stepanek**

Yoga and wellness services like massage often go hand in hand but are not always available together. Partner with a local Yoga, Pilates or fitness studio to give away free chair massage, skin care consultations or posture assessments at their location. If providing onsite samples or demonstrations is not an option, you could offer discount certificates towards your services for their clients to use at a future time. In exchange for whatever you provide, they could offer free trial classes or memberships for your clients. You may also find a way to partner joint advertising ventures in print media, direct mailings or online marketing.

Co-Host Events and Classes

Offer a class or host a speaker at your clinic or office on topics that would be of interest to your ideal clients or current clients as well as those of the other businesses you partner with. For example, in

January or February, host an event on Goal Setting and tie the program to any kind of "resolution" type service or product promotions you are offering. If the speaker is a Life Coach, they may want to use this as an introduction to a regular group meeting that helps people discover and achieve their goals that is hosted at (or sponsored by) your business. Invite everyone's clients to attend while sharing the expenses and responsibilities for the event.

This is a great way to bring new people in your doors and to keep your current client list engaged and involved with your business. It also helps clients to see your business as a resource for learning and information, not just for relaxation and pampering.

How to get started: Do some research on local speakers or professionals that would be appropriate for these types of seminars. You might also make a list of topics that you think would be of value to your clients throughout the year and then survey them to see what they are most interested in.

Community Involvement and Volunteering

Getting involved with causes you care about provides many opportunities besides just doing something good. It gives you a way to try new things, have fun with new people and grow as an individual. It can bring your practice local - and sometimes state-wide or national - goodwill and publicity. And as I mentioned in the section on Networking, it can even get you some new referrals and clients.

> "To me, giving back is so important. It makes others feel good which then in return makes me feel good."
>
> **Katie Cassidy**

Through my own businesses, I've been pretty involved in volunteering. For example, I've delivered Mobile Meals, collected relief supplies for those affected by Hurricane Katrina, and been "locked up" for the Muscular Dystrophy Association. They've all been feel-good win-win efforts for sure.

But the joy of volunteering doesn't end with raising money or awareness for these charities. It will also make you a better person and help you to appreciate all the blessings in your life and career. There's a lot of value in that! I encourage you to find a cause or organization you feel passionately about and begin brainstorming about the ways you can partner with them as an individual or business.

What causes are important to you that could also be a source of new clients?

_____

_____

_____

_____

Cooperative Competition

> "Competition has been shown to be useful up to a certain point and no further, but cooperation, which is the thing we must strive for today, begins where competition leaves off."
>
> **Franklin D. Roosevelt**

As you may have gathered from the section about networking with your competitors, I've been a big believer of "cooperative competition" as long as I've been in practice. I continue to encourage and welcome it to this day in all aspects of my businesses. Not only are there enough overall clients out there for all of us, but I believe there are plenty of ideal clients for each person's style of practice, personality and overall preferences.

That is not to say that everyone WILL have enough clients but, in my opinion, this is not due to too much competition. Rather, some people are not quite ready to succeed in their careers or perhaps are in the wrong business or area. Still others are just not be doing what they need to do to market, build and sustain a thriving business.

So why not do something in the spirit of cooperative competition? Form a support or networking group for area massage and spa professionals as suggesting in the section on *Networking?* Offer to host the first meeting at your office and give everyone a grand tour along with an explanation of your featured services and products. Use the time to get to know one another, solve common problems, discuss hiring practices and be sounding boards for your local colleagues and business owners. Try to meet once a month or quarter, perhaps each time at a different person's business.

Or if you want to keep it really simple, call up a competitor and invite them to trade services with you – or simply to have lunch. Regardless of what you choose, you'll likely some of the best business contacts possible...because they truly know and understand what you go through every day.

> "We must keep on trying to solve problems, one by one, stage by stage, if not on the basis of confidence and cooperation, at least on that of mutual toleration and self-interest."
>
> **Lester B. Pearson**

Strategy #7 - Your Website and Online Marketing

Having a well crafted, easy to navigate website is another extremely important marketing vehicle for your business. You can use it to promote and market your business to new clients while engaging your existing clients in a number of ways, some of which are described below. That being said, it is really important to understand a few key things about your website before getting started.

Start by having a domain name (website address) that is in line with your business name or tagline. Keep it as short and memorable as possible. If your business name is Pebble Beach Massage, try for www.PebbleBeachMassage.com or www.PebbleBeachMT.com. You'll also want to use a .com domain for your website if possible. True there are options out there like .net, .biz and .org. but most people instinctively gravitate to or type in .com addresses. Also, try not to have any dashes (-) or underscores (_) or unusual spellings in the domain name if possible as people don't remember these and then cannot find your site. In other words, pick a domain name that is simple to find, type and share!

> "Human nature has a tendency to admire complexity but reward simplicity."
>
> **Ben Huh**

Here's an example of what not to do:

www.myfavoritedayspa-atmrytlebeach.org.

Though constructing a website is pretty much a necessity these days, having a website without telling people about it is like putting a billboard out in the middle of the desert. For the most part no one sees it and it becomes a wasted investment of your marketing dollars. Thus you must promote your website to get people there.

Put your web address on everything you can from your front door and business cards to your mailing labels, checks, brochures, register receipts and email signature. Help people to find and remember it easily by sharing it everywhere you can. Invite your clients to go there often to see what's new, learn about upcoming specials or share testimonials about your business.

Additionally, make finding your brick and mortar business easy through your website! Be sure your full business address - including city & state – link to email and phone number are on every page of your site (unless you don't want clients to know where you are or how to reach you.) A map or link to your business or address on mapquest.com is also a nice touch.

To make doing business with you even easier, make sure the information on your site is complete. Include service descriptions and prices on your menu page(s). Offer online gift certificates, online appointments and perhaps a shopping cart for products. Don't make people work hard to buy, book or contact you or they will go somewhere else.

> "Search engine marketing and search engine optimization are critically important to online businesses. You can spend every penny you have on a website, but it will all be for nothing if nobody knows your site is there."
>
> **Marc Ostrofsky**

You'll also want to have a plan for engaging your clients directly on your website. You want people to read beyond the front page and find numerous ways to connecting with you as this connection helps to eventually win their trust, loyalty and business. The longer people stay on your site, the more likely they are to try out your services or business.

Some ideas of things to include to make your website more engaging and effective as a marketing tool:

- Online gift certificates - This really is a must! It increases your sales, appointments as well as your contact list and overall marketing opportunities.

- Online appointment booking - This makes scheduling easy especially for those who want to book an appointment NOW while they are online or using their smart phone. It's like having a receptionist 24/7!

- Online Shopping Cart – This is available through many client management software programs and can be linked to your site for online product sales and easy email marketing. If it's web-based, it also keeps you and your staff in touch with your client files and schedule easily.

- Articles or videos about stress reduction, healthy living – This shows your expertise and knowledge and can give your clients answers and information when they want it.

- Images of you, your location and treatments - People want to see what they are buying.

- Testimonials – These create positive word of mouth and show your credibility and reputation.

- Sign up form for email or text updates on specials, upcoming events or new products. This puts interested clients into a contact list that you can reach out to again and again.

- Sign up form for auto responders that deliver white papers, special reports, or free relevant tips on health and wellness. This is often used for more in-depth services or expensive procedures such as cosmetic treatments, laser hair removal and helps to pre-qualify potential candidates.

To make your site easier to find through web searches, you will also want use Search Engine Optimization (SEO) as a part of the building process. This gets your web site seen more often by search engines and as a result, your clients and prospects. There are others ways to do this which are too complex for me to explain here, especially since I am not a web professional. However, you can begin to get your site headed to the top of Google and AOL searches by doing a few key things.

> "SEO is a marketing function for sure, but it needs to be baked into a product, not slapped on like icing after the cake is baked."
>
> **Duane Forrester**

- ✓ Have strong descriptions, keywords and content

- ✓ Make the site easy to find, read and follow

- ✓ Update your content regularly

If you are a novice in this area or need help understanding SEO, talk to your web designer about how you can make sure your site is doing everything right in this area. Companies like LocalLighthouse.com can also help to create a secondary website that is fully optimized and will drive traffic to your main site and business. (If you contact them, please mention that my company, A to Zen Massage sent you!)

To insure your website is working properly, ask a few friends, colleagues or staff members to evaluate your website and other online marketing tools (appointment booking, gift certificate, store, etc) before sharing it with the general public.

Ask them to rate you in a few key areas.....

✓ Is it easy to use/understand/navigate?

✓ How easily could they find the information they wanted?

✓ How easy was it to contact you from the website?

✓ How easy was it to book an appointment?

✓ Does it look professional?

✓ Where does it need improvement?

Once your website is up and running, make sure to get it listed on a variety of online directories such as www.yp.com, www.CitySearch.com and www.Yelp.com. Many of these directories – like Yelp - also allow for consumer reviews of spa and wellness businesses. Depending on your business, there are a variety of other listing sites out there such as HealthProfs.com that are more targeted to clients looking for health, wellness or relaxation based services.

> "If the web is indeed a place, it is starting to look less like a library, and more like a river."
>
> **Peter Da Vanzo**

Periodically, do a Google search to find any new ones you are listed on and to make sure your profiles are complete and link back to your website. Then invite your clients to post some (hopefully positive) comments about you and their experiences at your business. You can make the most of the positive reviews by sharing or linking them on your website, blog, or Facebook page.

Email

Email is one of the simplest and most affordable tools for staying in touch with and marketing to clients. To be truly effective with it, there are a number of guidelines you should follow.

First of all, you need to think of your email signature as a marketing tool. It should contain your name and title, business name, direct contact details and any other pertinent information you want clients to see such as a link to schedule appointments.

I also like to encourage sales with hot links that say things like "Online Gift Certificates Now Available" or short client testimonials that sings my praises. A complete email signature can increase your sales and help people to find your website or business so much more easily! Better yet, it costs nothing to change or update.

When setting up email for your company, make sure you and your team have email addresses that agree with or match your domain name. It is not professional looking or effective for business owners or other spa or wellness pros to use a generic email address like SallySue@yahoo.com or IRubU@att.net for their business. Make sure your email has your first and/or last name AT your website's domain.

Example: My primary website is www.Spalutions.com and my email is Felicia@spalutions.com

Email Newsletters

Whether you've been out of touch for a while or just want to find an affordable way to communicate with clients, email newsletters can be a good way to share information and

> "The best ideas come as jokes. Make your thinking as funny as possible."
>
> **David Ogilvy**

updates on what you've been doing.

Look at how you communicate with clients and what you send out by email. Is it all about "buy buy buy"? Or is there anything of use FOR them, anything that expresses gratitude TO them or builds the relationship WITH them in what you relate. Whether you write once a week or once a month, aim to be consistent in your communications ☺

Do what you can to make your email marketing a little more personal so clients connect with you on a deeper level. Share a personal experience, a photo of your pet or kids, or simply a heartfelt message of appreciation. It makes the newsletter more interesting and effective, evokes warm feelings and helps create a more personal relationship with your clients.

Also, edit your email newsletter and other marketing materials (website, email signature, brochure, ads, etc) for consistency in terms of contact information. Do they all show your correct business name, website address, phone number, email, social media icons, etc? If not, note what is incorrect or missing and fix the omissions or errors.

Obviously, you'll also want to check for typos or bad grammar in any outgoing communications including email newsletters. If an error or misspelling is a one-time event, it may not do major damage. However, double and triple check all written, e-mailed and online text prior to sending it out to your customers to make the best electronic and written impressions possible.

Strategy #8 - Social Media – Social Networking

One of the most revolutionary things to hit marketing in the last few years is the use of social media. Whether you own your massage practice or work for someone else, learning how to promote yourself and your services through these twenty-first century portals is a vital step (in my opinion) to thrive and keep up with your competitors. If not, you may miss many fantastic opportunity to get the word out about your business and create what many marketing and PR professionals people call " buzz" – another key ingredient to a successful enterprise.

While I can't promise that joining any specific social media sites will bring all the new clients you want into your practice – they do provide you with a free way to stay connected with people you already know, announce events or new services, and even add a higher level of credibility to your career if used properly. All of these things can translate into more appointments and revenue.

> "Today's marketing success comes from self-publishing Web content that people want to share. It's not about gimmicks. It's not about paying an agency to interrupt others."
>
> **David Meerman Scott**

Though I'll discuss specific social media strategies, sites and tools in an upcoming volume of this series, it is important to understand why social media is a valuable asset and tool for your business.

Some specific benefits of using social media:

1) Increases communication and improves relationships with your clients and prospects.
2) Broadens your reach. The more people you know, the more you can reach through them to other clients and prospects.

3) Helps you establish yourself as an expert or resource in your area/field.

4) Assists you in tracking customer reviews and what is being said about your business

5) Brings a sense of fun into your business!

6) Drives traffic to your website and business.

7) Helps you get and keep more clients, increase sales AND improve your bottom line!

When using social media to market your business or practice, only reach out to people you know or have at least conversed with online. Do not farm other's lists or spam strangers to join your pages or groups.

If there is a business with a similar clientele or target market, approach them about doing some cross promotions or brainstorming on how you can help each other. Essentially you want to attract people to who are interested in what you do/say - not track them down and force them into hearing it!

> "To utilize social media tools effectively and properly, you must absolutely generate spontaneous communications in direct response to what others are saying or to what is happening in that moment. Be yourself. Be conversational. Be engaged."
>
> **Aliza Sherman**

If you are going to reach out to people you don't personally know on social networks but perhaps have some kind of connection such as a mutual friend, a group you both belong to, or a common interest, tell them about it when you try to connect so they understand why you are making contact. It will begin the relationship more smoothly.

One way to get started with social media is to take part in some of the online groups for massage, spa and wellness professionals. There are tons of them on Facebook and Linked In. These groups provide a chance to connect with other peers and professionals in the spa, salon and healing arts fields, ask questions, learn and become a part of the discussion. Start by joining Every Touch Marketing Group on Facebook and sharing your marketing tips and tricks☺ Go to https://www.facebook.com/groups/EveryTouchMarketing/ and ask to join.

As you are getting involved in the various sites and tools available, be sure to think before you post. Digital quotes and photos can be shared globally for their merit or their controversy. This can affect your business' success or struggle, especially if your clients, colleagues or competitors see it. So if you don't want your grandmother or boss to read it, don't write it. Instead, get a paper journal to record your rantings and grumbles. At least you can burn that someday! ☺

> "Don't say anything online that you wouldn't want plastered on a billboard with your face on it."
>
> **Erin Bury**

As with other marketing, if you promote yourself with social media, you'll want to track the results from your social media efforts. For example, on Facebook, you can track how many followers you've gained, who they are in terms of demographics and which posts have had the most views by visiting the Insights section. (This is currently at the top of your Fan Page and is one of the reasons to use fan pages - which are designed for business use - instead of using personal profile pages for business.)

Save yourself some time and effort by cross-linking your different social media tools and profiles. It's not that hard to do and can keep you from having to make duplicate posts every time you have news, open appointments or specials to share. For example, if you write a blog, get it set up as a Networked Blog on Facebook and set it to feed into your profile or fan page. You can also use tools like Crosspost Sharing Widgets (http://www.symphonytools.com/widgets) or Hootsuite (www.Hootsuite.com) to automate a lot of your social media.

One social media tool I use a lot is texting. According to a study by Edison Research, about 70% of Americans send and receive texts or SMS (short message service) messages via mobile phone - 45% doing so multiple times every day. I send many of my clients last minute appointment times this way which really keeps my schedule full. Take a look at how you can include text or SMS messaging in your own marketing efforts. And there are services and point of sale programs that can automate this process for you.

I referred to online reviews in the previous section on *Your Website and Online Marketing.* Though we hope and pray for only positive reviews for our businesses, some negative comments are bound to show up from time to time. Learn to use negative online reviews or complaints as a chance for positive PR by responding to them in an upbeat, proactive way.

> "Conversations among the members of your marketplace happen whether you like it or not. Good marketing encourages the right sort of conversations."
>
> **Seth Godin**

On the same site(s) as the complaints, invite the person who made them back for a return visit or explain how you have fixed the problem since their visit. It shows you are actively concerned about your business and level of customer service. Doing this also spreads a good word about your business and encourages other clients and fans to share their experiences as well.

To keep up with negative reviews and other online comments or links shared about your business, track what people are saying with Google

90

Alerts. If you've got a Google account, just log-in and then select "Alerts" from the menu. Set one up for your business name, web or blog address, or even yourself. Get updates as things are posted for the most up-to-the-minute info or once a week if that update timeframe suits you better. Read each link and make sure it's framing your business in a good one and respond as needed.

Blogging

Become a thought leader in your area and industry. How? One way is to start a blog (aka "web log") where you share information that is helpful and relevant to your clients. From seasonal skin care advice to relaxation or make-up tips, you and your staff have plenty of information to pass on. One suggestion: start a blog only if you are able to commit posting at least once or twice a week.

> "The key with blogging is to lay it all out there because sooner or later people are going to know what you know, so might as well be the first one to share the information and get credit for it."
>
> **Neil Patel**

Blogging actually combines website marketing with social media and most blogs are hosted on your own web site. Use this popular forum to discuss spa-related issues, new products or services you've been hearing about, customer service issues, etc. You could also open it up to questions from your clients and offer answers to their queries on a daily or weekly basis. The idea is to find ways to get people on your site (and hopefully in your doors) spending money repeatedly. If you are more interested in discussing professional issues and problems, you may want to join a spa-related chat group instead.

Blogs are also a great place for posting pictures and videos, newsfeeds about spa, wellness or relaxation related issues, media info about the product lines you carry and more. Write articles and share videos or other resources that will assist your ideal clients in solving their problems. Don't just make it an ongoing sales pitch about your business. While you can alert people about specials, classes, new services, etc., the primary content should be educational, entertaining, engaging or just plain helpful.

One really cool thing about blogs is the constant exposure they bring your business on the web. Since search engines like Google and Yahoo are always searching for new content, blogs can help your web site rankings move up on the charts, bringing even more business in your doors.

> "Today people don't trust companies. One of the things marketers want to do is to humanize their brand. What better way to do it than put a live person in front of them?"
>
> **Jackie Huba**

Here are some simple ways to get started:

- Start a blog that shares relevant information or thoughts with your clients and prospects. A blog is sometimes like a journal, so it can be a little off the topic of your business and provides a way for people to learn about you, your company and industry. As with any social media, be aware that you should *only* write in it what you don't mind the entire world knowing about you.

- Comment on other people's blogs. Write from your professional perspective when appropriate or possible and include info about your business (name, web site and/or email address) so that people can follow up with you if they want to. Look for blogs that relate to your profession, area or subjects that interest you.

- Take advantage of the effortless broadcasting abilities of YouTube and post a video on your blog of something your clients or potential clients will be interested in. This could be a makeup lesson, reflexology demonstration, or even some video testimonials from clients (or staff) about why they love your spa or practice. Have fun, be creative and also share the link to the video blog in your next email newsletter. For shorter looping videos, check out Vine (www.Vine.co).

- If you've always wanted to have a blog but just don't know what to say in 400 words or more, start with Twitter, a site for micro-blogging in 140 characters or less. Share your favorite quotes, links to articles, updates on open appointments or announcements for new products. Hint: whenever possible, drive your followers/traffic to your own website, full blog, other social media sites and business.

Done right, blogging can be a great way to establish yourself as an expert in your field; create understanding about what you do; grow relationships with clients and prospects; and even be a fun creative outlet for you.

Golden Rules of Blogging

✓ Use good headlines

✓ Share relevant information

✓ Leave out the jargon

✓ Include links, photos & videos

✓ Keep the blog up to date, fun and interesting.

✓ Cross-link with other SM

✓ Keep it short, sweet & scan-able!

✓ And make sure your clients know about it!

Other Ideas to Get New Clients

- Be open to business whenever and wherever it finds you. I've booked numerous client appointments while out with friends because a) I had my appointment book with me or b) I knew my schedule off the top of my head and was able to book the session on the spot. Other times, I've also run into old clients I've lost touch with and invited them to come back. Later, I looked them up on Facebook and sent a message offering a new client rate to return;-)

- Make it easy for people to buy what you are marketing to them. Whether that means having an open schedule or an open attitude, the easier you make it to purchase from you, the more people will!

- Put something outside your business to draw the eye and/or walk-in traffic. This could include a sandwich board with today's specials or open appointments listed, a bunch of helium balloons or even a bubble blower. Go with what fits the tone and style of your spa or office. Be creative and have a little fun getting your company noticed in a whole new way.

- Consider using your car as a marketing "vehicle". Whether you add magnetic signage, a custom license plate, a vehicle wrap or just a bumper sticker promoting your business, your automobile is sure to get your business name out!

- While you're out and about or just in the business, promote the business with a logoed shirt, umbrella, water bottle or reusable shopping bag. Many of these can also be given to clients as thank you gifts as well as sold in your retail area.

- Talk to another business close-by to see if they will allow you to offer a gift certificate for a free or specially priced service in a drawing they hold for their clients. In the best case scenario, the other business will share the names and contact info of those who entered so you can continue marketing people who were interested to win your prize.

- Look through your current business contacts to see who you want to talk with about referrals, events, corporate gift certificates, cross promotions, etc. Then make a prioritized list of who to contact first, second, third, etc., along with specific goals or reason(s) for getting in touch. The people you know can valuable resources to help you reach new clients – so utilize them!

3 KEEPING CLIENTS THRU REBOOKING

With all the practical tips for getting new clients shared in the last chapter, you may already be making plans to invest all your marketing time and dollars on attracting new clients. It's an exciting prospect to come up with all the new tools and strategies available to connect with groups of your ideal clients.

But while it is important to keep an ongoing flow of new people coming through your door, it is equally if not more important to invest time and energy in getting each of those new clients to return over and over again.

> In marketing I've seen only one strategy that can't miss - and that is to market to your best customers first, your best prospects second and the rest of the world last.
>
> **John Romero**

Unfortunately, whether in practice for years or just getting started many massage, spa and wellness professionals don't always succeed at rebooking new clients and – at least periodically - find themselves with too many open appointment times on their hands because they failed to get their clients to reschedule. And while free time has certain advantages, having empty treatment rooms usually means having an empty bank account.

Asking and getting new and current clients to return to your business is a critical part of business development. Some people are resistant to this idea and have shared a number of reasons and excuses over the years including:

"I don't want to seem pushy."
"People will think I just want to make money"
"My clients should just call me when they are ready."

Excuses are easy to make and may seem realistic or logical when they are going through our minds. However, I'd like you to also consider the possibility that by not asking clients to rebook, you are sending the message that you don't want or need their business for some reason. They may also interpret the lack of an invitation to return as proof that they were a bad client.

> "Profit in business comes from repeat customers, customers that boast about your project or service, and that bring friends with them."
>
> **W. Edwards Deming**

These ideas may seem far-fetched to you at first. But consider your own reaction and feelings the last time you weren't invited to a party hosted by someone you considered a friend or not invited to return to a business you visited.

Like all of us, many of our clients have their own insecurities and may interpret your lack of interest in them returning as apathy towards them or evidence of an inability to meet their needs or solve their problems. They may feel insulted, assume that they did something wrong, or *think that you just didn't like them.*

Is that what you want?

I sincerely doubt it and hope this new perspective will open your eyes to the potentially negative impact NOT inviting clients to come back can have on your clients and your business. Besides, attracting new clients costs **five to seven times** the money and effort of what retaining business of existing clients does. Any more questions?

Let's now take a look at what the potential positive impact of rebooking a client and retaining their loyalty, referrals and business for the long-term can be.

Why Getting New Clients Alone is Not Enough
Lifetime Value of a Client –An Example

Client A/Abby

Average Service Cost	$65
Number of Visits per year	x 12
Subtotal	**= $780**
Average spent on Retail Purchases per year	+ $120
Average spent on Gift Certificates per year	+ $195
Subtotal	**=$1095**
How Many Years of Business	x 6

LIFETIME VALUE FOR CLIENT A/Abby   **$6,570**

Abby refers two friends that spend as much or more as she does.

Client B/Bruce

Average Service Cost	$65
Number of Visits per year	x 24
Subtotal	**= $1560**
Average spent on Retail Purchases per year	+ $360
Average spent on Gift Certificates per year	+ $390
Subtotal	**= $2310**
How Many Years of Business	5

LIFETIME VALUE FOR CLIENT B/Bruce   **$11,550**

Client C - Cathy

Average Service Cost	$90
Number of Visits per year	x 17
Subtotal	**= $1530**
Average spent on Retail Purchases per year	+ $850
Average spent on Gift Certificates per year	+ $500
Subtotal	**= $2880**
How Many Years of Business	x 10

LIFETIME VALUE FOR CLIENT C/Cathy   **$28,800**

Abby's TRUE Lifetime value is A+B+C = $46,920

Lifetime Value of Your Clients

Client A

Average Service Cost	_____
Number of Visits per year	x_____
Subtotal	=_____
Average spent on Retail Purchases per year	+_____
Average spent on Gift Certificates per year	+_____
Subtotal	=_____
How Many Years of Business	x_____

LIFETIME VALUE FOR CLIENT A   _____

Client A refers 2 friends that will spend as much or more as she does.

Client B

Average Service Cost	_____
Number of Visits per year	x_____
Subtotal	=_____
Average spent on Retail Purchases per year	+_____
Average spent on Gift Certificates per year	+_____
Subtotal	=_____
How Many Years of Business	x_____

LIFETIME VALUE FOR CLIENT B   _____

Client C

Average Service Cost	_____
Number of Visits per year	x_____
Subtotal	=_____
Average spent on Retail Purchases per year	+_____
Average spent on Gift Certificates per year	+_____
Subtotal	=_____
How Many Years of Business	x_____

LIFETIME VALUE FOR CLIENT C y   _____

Now what is the value of Client A?   (A+B+C)_____

<u>**Can you see the value of asking clients to rebook & refer others?!**</u>

Strategy #1 – Ask Clients to Rebook

Probably the easiest and most effective way I've found to keep my schedule not just full but overflowing is by consistently rebooking existing clients. Clearly, the best time to get a client to schedule another appointment is right after a service before they leave your business. They've just experienced your amazing skills and are sure to be enthusiastic about coming back. Not only that, but when you are face-to-face with your clients, you are able to discuss all the appointment possibilities and upcoming specials in person rather than over the phone, through voicemail, texts or emails.

Besides, if you always leave it to the client to call when they are ready to make another appointment, you run the great risk of the client *never* making that call. Even if they adore you, it could be literally YEARS before you hear from them again. So, the first step in getting clients to rebook is simply to ASK THEM. This may seem like an extremely simple strategy...and it is. But few service professionals take the time to do this one simple task consistently and with every client.

> "For every sale you miss because you're too enthusiastic, you will miss a hundred because you're not enthusiastic enough.
>
> Zig Ziglar

Begin asking <u>all</u> of your clients if they'd like to schedule their next appointment before they leave. Don't be shy...you can do it!

Script for Asking Clients to Rebook (after the appointment):

You: "How are you feeling, Jennifer?"

Client: "Wow. That facial was great. I feel wonderful."

You: "Oh I am so glad to hear that. Here is some water for you."

Client: "Thank you."

You: "Jennifer, you mentioned earlier when you checked in that you wanted to start getting facials regularly. Would you like to schedule your next appointment while you're here?"

Client: "Sure. I'd like to come back in about a month."

You: "Perfect. Four weeks from today is Friday February 26th. Allison, who you saw today, could see you for a Custom Facial at 2 or 3:30 PM. Which would you prefer?"

Client: "I'll take the 3:30 slot."

You: "Thanks Jennifer. That's Friday February 26th at 3:30 for a Custom Facial. If anything comes up or changes, please be sure to give at least 24 hours notice."

Client: "No problem. I'll see you then."

You: "Great. Have a great day!"

Strategy #2 – Explain the Benefits of Your Service

The first tip I mentioned is one of the simplest ways to get your clients to rebook...simply asking them to do so. But how do you convince a client that having another service with you is what they need or want to do? Again, if you don't ask them to reschedule while they're still in your business, other things will come probably up. Their time will be devoted to other activities...they'll forget how important or helpful your services are for them. By not rebooking

> "This may seem simple, but you need to give customers what they want, not what you think they want. And, if you do this, people will keep coming back."
>
> **John Ilhan**

your appointments, your business will probably end up with more than a few holes in its schedule. Here is a suggestion for getting your clients prepped and ready to reschedule.

Don't assume that clients know what benefits come from getting regular treatments. This is especially important if they are a new client or if this is their first exposure to your type of skills or service. Make sure to educate them on the normal amount of visits for their needs (once a week, once a month, quarterly) or what is generally an acceptable amount of time between appointments for each of the services they get from you.

Remind them of the importance of taking care of themselves, both physically and mentally, and how regular treatments are a vital part of both looking and feeling their best. I often explain that services like facials or massages are not only a pampering or relaxing indulgence, but also a necessity for your skin and body, just like regular oil changes and maintenance are for your car. This is especially true if the clients have a particular concern or problem that they are seeking treatment for.

Begin by making a list of the benefits of each of the services you offer and begin telling all clients about those benefits and why they should come in regularly.

Script for Explaining the Benefits of Your Service:

You: "Well David, since this is your first massage with me, I just wanted to see if you had any questions about what I will be doing or about massage in general."

Client: "Actually I am curious about the benefits of massage. I've had one before and it felt really good. But I'm not sure what massage does or helps."

You: "Well, among other things, massage elicits a feeling of calm and well being and can reduce some types of anxiety and depression. It also helps you to move better and makes you feel cared for, safe and comfortable. Massage may also help decrease inflammation in muscles and may effectively reduce or eliminate back pain. And like you said, it feels great, which I think is the biggest benefit of all."

Client; "Wow. I had no idea massage did so much."

You: "Yes, massage does a lot for you. Most massage clients tell us they can really feel a difference in their aches and pains as well as their outlook when they get regular massage. They use it for "personal maintenance" just like you would by getting oil changes for your car. Getting a massage every once in awhile is good, but having one every week or month is even better."

Strategy #3 – Identify Your Clients Needs

Now that you're telling your clients the benefits of your services and asking them to rebook each and every time they check out, let's take things one step further by making the entire service experience client-focused. The goal here is to meet their needs and expectations so that they'll feel totally taken care of and ready to come back.

Hopefully you are already getting some type of client intake or health history form filled out at the client's first visit. This form you should get a good idea of why the client is there to see you. That being said, asking why someone is there at each visit usually leads to a better outcome during and after the session. Whether it is for

> "The aim of marketing is to know and understand the customer so well the product or service fits him and sells itself."
>
> **Peter Drucker**

pampering, relaxation, a particular condition, or a special occasion you will be better prepared to make their experience the best possible, creating a higher value, and a happier client!

Start to ask all of your clients what they need or want from their appointment at the beginning of each session. Then do your best to fulfill their requests, solve their problems and serve their needs.

Script #1 for Identifying Your Clients' Needs:

You: "It's wonderful to see you again, Heather. Let's chat for a minute before we begin your session."

Client: "Sure."

You: "I know you usually get a manicure and pedicure when you come in. Is there any reason you decided not to schedule both this time?"

Client: "Well actually I'm really rushed today and only have time for the pedicure. In fact I really don't have time for that."

You: "Thanks Heather. I'm so glad you told me that you were in a hurry. Would it be helpful to you if we finished a few minutes early?"

Client: "That would be great. Can we do that without much trouble?"

You: "Sure. I'd be glad to shorten or even skip the manicure today entirely if that would help you get out on time."

Client: "That sounds great. I didn't know you could shorten those steps."

You: "Yes and it's no problem. The next time I see you I'll be glad to do some extra massage during your services. Now let's get started!"

Script # 2 for Identifying Your Clients' Needs:

You: "Jack, I see on your intake form that you want your neck, shoulders, chest and back to be addresses in today's waxing session. However, we only have 30 minutes planned which is not enough for all those areas. Would it be OK if I just wax your back today and do the other areas later? Or do you have another preference?"

Client: "You know my back is the biggest issue. I really would like to get that waxed today. Then next week maybe I can get everything else done."

Strategy #4 – Get Permission to Treat Clients Needs

So far we've talked about asking clients to rebook, educating them on the benefits of your services, and identifying their needs. What else can be done? Well, plenty actually. Try this next one out!

Once you have determined the specific reason(s) for a client's visit, pave the way for future service and product recommendations. Simply ask your clients if they would like you to provide information on services or products that can help them achieve their goals. This should take some of the hesitation out of the way for you to ask clients to come back again and again.

Take the time to revisit each of your client's pain relief, beauty, wellness or relaxation goals. As you begin each session, simply let them know that you want to give them the best service possible by finding out if they have any new concerns with their skin, hair, nails, body or overall health. After they answer, ask if you can give them recommendations to help them get the results they want.

> "Spend a lot of time talking to customers face to face. You'd be amazed how many companies don't listen to their customers."
>
> **Ross Perot**

Also, check in with your clients before each session. Don't assume they just want "the usual." Find out if they have any new concerns or problems since you last saw them. By knowing what specifically your client wants and needs each visit, you will be better able to help them meet their goals. Their ongoing satisfaction with you and your services should bring them in again and again.

As you work on incorporating this strategy, ask all your clients, but especially the new people you see, if it is OK for you to give them suggestions that can help them achieve their specific goals or resolve their problems. Then follow through on your recommendations, but only with things that truly are suited to their needs and goals.

Script #1 for Getting Permission to Treat Your Client's Needs:

You: "Sandra, it is so nice to meet you. Before we begin your massage I just wanted to ask you a few questions."

Client: "OK."

You: "Your client intake form mentions a concern you have about your skin being dry in addition to wanting to get some relief from your shoulder pain today."

Client: "Yes that's right. It seems like my skin just stays dry."

You: "That's good to know, Sandra. I actually offer a hydrating body wrap that can really help with dry skin. Is it OK with you if I suggest other services or home-care products that can help treat your skin dryness, shoulder pain or other issues that we might uncover?"

Client: "That would be great. I was really hoping you might have suggestions."

You: "Wonderful. Let's start with the massage. Then during the session, I'll try to evaluate if this body wrap would be a good thing to try. I may also give you some product recommendations that have worked for other clients. How does that sound?"

Client: "Wonderful. I am so glad I came to see you!"

Script #2 for Getting Permission to Treat Your Client's Needs:

You: "Susie, since you mentioned at your last appointment that you want to reduce the fine lines around your eyes, I'd like to suggest you try this new eye cream we got in. Here are the instructions for it."

Client: "Wow! Thank you for remembering what we talked about. I'm really excited to try the new product!"

Strategy #5 – Keep a Cancellation List

Each of the strategies shared so far will definitely add some repeat clients and appointments to your schedule. But what do you do for those days when you have unexpected openings or late cancellations? There are actually a number of ways to deal with this, but the most effective thing I ever did was to keep a cancellation list.

As I get to know my clients and determine if we are a good match for each other, and especially if they want to get massage on a regular basis, I also ask if they are interested in last minute appointment opportunities. Some people on my list actually never schedule appointments in advance but instead wait for that inevitable call from me...

> "You can't do today's job with yesterday's methods and be in business tomorrow."
>
> **Unknown**

"I had a cancellation for tomorrow at 4 PM...Can you make it?"

As you get busier and more in demand, this is also a great strategy for clients you just couldn't fit in anywhere as well as for those who can't schedule in advance.

Begin by making a list of your clients who have last minute flexibility for appointments. If you aren't sure who can do this, start asking clients as they come in or send out an email survey if they would be interested in this kind of update. Also keep an ongoing list of clients you weren't able to schedule for a particular time, day or service. Keep this by the appointment book or computer where you can easily access it. Review daily and use it when you get a cancellation!

Script for Keeping a Cancellation List:

You: "Julie, thank so much for coming in today. I really appreciate your business."

Client: "Oh the pleasure is all mine. You give the best body polishes."

You: "Well thanks. I'm so glad to hear that. By the way, I am starting a cancellation and last minute appointment list for my practice. Lately there've been a few late cancellations I've been unable to fill and I want to be better prepared. I know you schedule appointments regularly but don't have a set routine for coming in. Would you be interested in taking advantage of last minute appointment openings if we called you?"

Client: "Actually, I would be interested and so would my husband. We both work from home and have pretty flexible schedules."

You: "That great Julie. Are there any days or times that you prefer to come in or is anything fine?"

Client: "After 2 PM is probably the best for me, but my husband would probably prefer morning cancellations."

You: "Great. I will make a note of that in your file. Are you interested in appointments for body polishes only or for other services as well?"

Client: "Well, I've never had a body wrap or facial but I guess call me for whatever openings you get. That might give me a reason to try something new out!"

You: "OK. I'll put you down for both as well as your husband."

Client: "That sounds good. Thanks so much for asking about that. Maybe it will help us both out!"

Strategy #6 – Offer to Set Up Standing Appointments

Once you determine a client is interested in receiving your services on a regular basis, suggest setting up regular or standing appointments. Explain how busy you're becoming and as a thank you for being a regular client, you would like to give them priority on your schedule. This is a nice time-saving service for them that guarantees income for you while also making them feel like a VIP.

Work together to select regular weekly, bi-weekly or monthly times. Then block that time out for an agreed upon period of time – perhaps a year – or even indefinitely. And if you find at a later time that the chosen time is not working for some reason, talk with your client about finding another time slot or going back to scheduling individual appointments.

> "Perfection has to do with the end product, but excellence has to do with the process."
>
> **Jerry Moran**

Script for *Setting Up Standing Appointments*:

You: "Hi Mike. Thanks for coming in today! I really enjoyed working with you again."

Client: *"Thanks. I really enjoy coming to see you for facials."*

You: "Wonderful. I'm really glad you do. Thanks to regulars like you and referrals I've been getting, my schedule is getting busier and busier. Since you have been such a good client, I'd like to offer you a standing appointment for your facials so that you don't miss out on your preferred appointment day and time."

Client: *"Hmm, that sounds interesting. How would that work?"*

You: "Well, we would determine the best day and time for your session as well as the frequency of your appointments? You've been

111

coming in about once a month, so we could set your time up for every four weeks. Would that be best for you?"

Client: "That would work well if I could set it up on Tuesdays at 4 pm or later."

You: "Great. It looks like I can do every fourth Tuesday at 4PM for a Men's Facial. If it suits you, we can start that with your next appointment on Tuesday March 2nd. Will that work?"

Client: "That will be fine. One question though. What if I need to change or cancel my appointment?"

You: "That's no problem. You can change or cancel your standing appointments with 24 hours notice just like you have in the past. The only real difference is that your time is reserved for you on a standing basis without you needing to schedule it each and every month."

Client: "OK. That sounds good. Thanks so much for suggesting that. I think that will definitely make my life a little easier."

Strategy #7 – Have a System for Client Follow-Up

Whether you decide to call each new client after their first visit, send a hand-written thank you card, or simply send a quick email note, making contact with each new customer as well as regular clients after a session can go quite a way toward creating a long lasting professional relationship with them.

Like most other marketing efforts, it is helpful to have a specific system or plan in place for how you follow up with clients. For example, as they are resting on the table after their appointment, you might go ahead and fill out the thank you note you plan to drop in the mail the next day. Or you may prefer to set aside a few minutes each morning or afternoon to place quick calls to all new clients you saw the day before or those who may have tried a new service or technique.

> "The well-satisfied customer will bring the repeat sale that counts."
>
> **James Cash Penney**

Determine what types of follow up work best for you including phone calls, hand written notes or postcards, emails or even text messages. Then plan a time each day or week to follow up or "check in" with new and repeat clients. Be sure to have your schedule handy in case anyone needs to change or add an appointment on the spot.

If you use client management software or a point of sale system like MindBodyOnline or SpaBooker, auto emails can also be set up to be sent a day or two after a clients first visit as can surveys about what they liked most or would choose to improve about their visit.

Script #1 for Client Follow Up (message):

"Hi Susan. This is Dexter from Massage Madness. I just wanted to check in and see how you were feeling after the Lomi Lomi Massage we did yesterday. You

can reach us at 333-222-1111 with any comments, questions or to schedule your next appointment. It was my pleasure to meet you and I hope to see you again very soon!"

Sample Text for Client Follow Up (note):

Dear Matt –

Thank you so much for visiting Relaxation Vacation Day Spa last week. I really appreciate your business and look forward to your return on Tuesday March 10th at 6PM for a Hot and Cold Stone Facial. Until then, please remember that we want more clients just like you and reward your referrals with a $10 credit towards any service.

Thanks again for your business. Keep relaxing!

Sincerely -

Sandy Smith
Owner – Relaxation Vacation Day Spa

Strategy #8 – Create a Treatment Plan for Each Client

Earlier in this section, I discussed *Determining Your Clients' Needs* and *Getting Permission to Treat Your Clients' Needs*. What was missing from those two suggestions was actually creating a treatment plan for each client and sharing it with them.

To set a successful treatment plan, you need to be aware of each client's goals, needs or expectations for their visit. By defining this and getting permission to share other information that will help them solve their problem, you are laying the foundation for creating a treatment plan.

Unfortunately, some massage, spa and wellness professionals shy away from doing this. They are afraid that by telling their clients how often they need to come in or how many sessions it is likely to take to help improve a particular condition, they are "prescribing" or somehow stepping out of their scope of practice. The truth is that most clients seek out your services as a solution to a problem. Whether they want to look better, feel better, get rid of their pain, fight aging, or de-stress, they are looking to you for answers. And, as a professional, it is your job to advise them on what you know best – how your services and/or products can help them find the solution they are looking for.

> "To find out what the customer needs you have to understand what the customer is doing as well as he understands it. Then you build what he needs and you educate him to the fact that he needs it."
>
> **Edna St. Vincent Millay**

Practice discussing and recommending treatment plans to a co-worker, friend, spouse, or even to yourself while looking in the mirror. Think about how often you would recommend the services you offer to clients for some of your niche or specialty areas. For example, I always tell relaxation-seeking clients that a great rule of thumb for the frequency of getting massage is once a month if they can't fit it into their schedule or budget more often.

Script for Creating a Treatment Plan for Each Client:

You: "Mary, to improve the fine lines you have concerns about, I suggest you come in weekly for the next six weeks for a series of chemical peels. Is there a time that works for you next Friday?"

Mary: "Sure. I can come in at 2 PM."

You: "Perfect. We can just do the peel for the first five weeks and then schedule another Deep Treat Facial on the sixth week. After that, if you are happy with the results we can do a peel every four to six weeks when you come in for your Facial. How does that sound? "

Mary: "I think I can do that. Would it be ok if I got another facial in four weeks though?

You: "Sure that will be fine and will help to provide extra hydration for your skin. We'll see what makes sense for scheduling your next facial after that."

Mary: "Great. I find your facials so relaxing that I really want to get one once a month."

Strategy #9 – Set an Example and Get More Services!

How great is this for a marketing strategy? I think it is vitally important for you to practice what you preach *by receiving the services you promote and provide* to your clients on a regular basis.

As a full-time massage therapist, I have ALWAYS set an example by getting a massage at a bare minimum of once a month – and when I was first in practice at least once a week. It's great marketing to be able to share this when clients ask about the suggested frequency of visits and can often lead to them booking sooner than planned. Besides, how can any wellness professional expect their clients to come in regularly if they are not taking care of themselves in the same way they recommend?

> "My father taught me that the only way you can make good at anything is to practice, and then practice some more."
>
> **Pete Rose**

Schedule an appointment TODAY for whatever services you provide – especially those that fill YOU up with energy, excitement and passion for what you do – so that you can look and feel as great as your clients do. You'll feel better and remember exactly why your clients should come in more often!

Script for *Getting Services Regularly*:

Spa of your choice: "Thank you for calling ABC Spa. How can I help you?"

You: "I'd like to schedule a (fill-in your service of choice) please."

Spa of your choice: "Wonderful. When would you like to come in?"

You: "At least once or twice a month all year long!"

Other Rebooking Ideas

- Pick up the phone and call a long lost client just to say hello and reconnect. Find out how they are, what they've been up to and let them know you miss seeing them. Keep the call light and casual but feel free to end with a reminder that you're still open, around and would love to work with them again. If you're too shy to do this by phone, send them a note or email to reconnect.

- Have a plan for how you follow up with clients that you haven't seen in a while. Lots of client management software programs can sort your database in all kinds of ways including the date of their last visit. Pull your list and then get to emailing, phoning or mailing those folks with an offer to get them back in.

- Consider creating a new client welcome kit. Include things like your brochure, policies and business card along with promotional items (magnet, water bottle, canvas bag), product samples, coupons for future services, referral cards and other goodies. Be sure the bag has your logo, website and contact information on it - and that you invite each client back as you give them one.

- Start a VIP Club. Similar to a loyalty program, this group should be limited to your biggest spenders or most loyal clients and can offer special rates, advance notice of open appointments, VIP only events, etc. You may want to base membership on how much someone spends annually, how many visits they have per year, the number of referrals sent, length of time as a customer or all of the above. The key is to do things for your VIPs that makes these folks feel very special and appreciated for supporting your business over the long-term.

- When offering a client appointment options, always provide an either/or choice as opposed to a yes/no choice. Also, guide people to your less busy times first to see if they can take them. *"David, I have several times open the week of August 16th. Would Monday or Tuesday work for you? I have 10 or 11:30 am open both days."* Your schedule is NEVER completely open! :-)

- If a client can't rebook while they are still in the office, offer to contact them at a future time when they have their calendar handy. *"Janice, since you don't have your calendar, I'd be glad to call or email you in a few weeks with some open days and times. When is the best time to get in touch?"* Some will say no, but many will think you are awesome for providing this extra service.

- Let people know how much you enjoy working with them and ask every single client you see to rebook. *"Sarah, it was so nice to meet you. I am accepting new clients and would love to see you again. Would you like to schedule another appointment while you are here? I usually work Tuesday through Saturday from 10-6."* Try it!

- When your clients do want to rebook their next appointment, do your best to guide them through the process. *"Max, I know you mentioned wanting to get services regularly. I generally suggest clients come in at least once every four to six weeks. Will that work for you?"* Then take a look at specific days or times that are open for both of you in the desired time frame.

4 CONCLUSION

Remember, it takes a lot of hard work and perseverance to build and keep a clientele. And no matter what you do, there will still be times when your appointment book and office are less than full. Even the most talented, in-demand professionals in the world occasionally have a slow day.

However, if you are clear about your goals, strive to provide the best possible experience to your ideal clients and follow through with each person you see in the ways suggested in this book, you are bound to become and stay as busy as you want to be.

Some other thoughts...

- Have passion for what you do and sell. Period.

- Know your marketing goals and ideal clients. Get clear on what you are trying to accomplish, sell or promote AND who you intend to reach with your marketing.

- Look at your business goals and assess if your current marketing activities are in line with them. For example, if your goal is to see ten new clients a week but you are not asking existing clients for referrals, you may have a problem reaching your goal. Or if you want to sell $500 in products per week, but have no incentives for your staff to sell or no inventory in stock, it may be hard to reach the goal.

- Simplify and make your marketing "all about the client." Sell results and benefits, not just how wonderful you, your facility, training or staff members are. People buy because they understand what's in it for them. Know your clients, what they want to buy, and where they look for information about their potential purchases.

- Clients buy solutions and results. Become a problem solver and teach your staff to sell solutions to problems rather than just the products and services you offer. Go through your list of services/products and list the kinds of issues they can help and/or what results they offer. Then train your staff to talk about how your offerings solve certain problems or provide specific results.

- Share information about your business in a variety of ways. Engage people about current promotions when you talk to them on the phone or they come for an appointment. Post signs. Send emails. Use social media. Spread the word.

- Whatever marketing actions you take, give them enough time to be successful. Example, if you go to a new networking group/meeting, do you just visit one time and base your success/fail rate off that visit? Or do you go at least three times to make your face familiar and presence known? Consistency and repetition make marketing more effective!

- Make time for marketing or dedicated business development on your schedule each day or week. Block off an hour in the morning, evening or whenever you are best able to focus. That time is ONLY for business development - nothing else.

Example: I attend to social media and general follow up for about an hour first thing each day. I also schedule a writing or office day at least once or twice a week to work on my blogs and larger outreach projects. Have a specific "to do" list for what you want to accomplish in that time. If you aren't sure, take on the task that will bring you the most money first, like calling people on your cancellation list.

- Reclaim your energy! Find the number one thing on your "to do" list or desk that is distracting you and keeping you from promoting or growing your business the way you really want to. Then do it, delegate it or ditch it so you can get focused on the things that will help your company or practice grow.

- From time to time, take a break from all the brainstorming, strategizing and planning about marketing and growing your business to just be. Clearing your mind of clutter and your calendar of "to-do's" can actually be one of the most productive and creative ways to move your business forward. If you haven't done it lately, schedule some "do nothing" time ASAP! ☺

- Remember that marketing is *a process*, not a one-time occurrence. Repetition is another important factor in successful marketing. You may think people saw the ONE email you sent or ad you ran about your new service, but it's likely most of them didn't. Keep putting it out there.

- Be patient with yourself and *the process* as you launch a new product or service, work to build a clientele or create the brand of your business. Though your hard work and enthusiasm can make it happen, success will not come overnight. So take a deep breath and be grateful for where things are now as well what will come.

- Similarly, as a part of being persistent, you'll want to devise systems for creating consistency in all of your marketing efforts. Otherwise a lot of your hard work, energy and investment in making the connections could be wasted!

- TAKE ACTION today and EVERY day in some way to market yourself and your business. The greatest ideas do not succeed if they are only in your head. Make them real by trying them out. And take to heart the wise words of Henry Ford: *"It has been my observation that most people get ahead during the time that others waste time."*

- Don't be afraid to try something new in your marketing or your business just because it might fail. Failing is part of learning and succeeding. Thus every failure brings you closer to success and getting what you want. If you aren't failing, it might be because you aren't trying. Your marketing doesn't have to be perfect. What matters most is that you DO IT! From there take the results or feedback you get to continually improve your efforts and keep moving forward!

RESOURCES AND SPECIAL OFFERS

FREE ONLINE RESOURCES – Go to www.EveryTouchMarketing.com and order the instant download of *ETM Resources for Volume 1* which includes expanded versions of all worksheets. Use the code **VOLUME1** to get them FREE☺

From Massage Office Software...

More Offers >>>>>>>>>>

Schedulicity - Today's leading service professionals have full control over their calendar and they also make it accessible to their customers – 24/7. Schedulicity will elevate your business and make life easier for you and your clients. Use the promo code SMARTSPA at www.Schedulicity.com to get a 60 day trial!

Spa Boom - Bring the brand experience of your spa online with SpaBoom's low-cost, high-power tools. Easily craft your online marketing and produce significant, measurable results with SpaBoom's low-cost, high-power tools. Go to www.SpaBoom.com/spalutions for special offers and pricing.

Spa Time Now - Get the first month free for the basic or enhanced listings on www.SpaTimeNow.com when you use the promo code SMARTSPA

Gift Card Café – Online gift certificates made affordable and easy. Go to this link to sign up: http://www.thegiftcardcafe.com/affiliateLink.php?affID=78

Easy Salon Newsletters - Easy Salon Newsletters is a fully customizable "done-for-you" print and email newsletter service for salons, spas, and medi spas. There are 4 subscription levels. Get a free month trial, $107 value. Satisfaction guaranteed. Go to www.EasySalon Newsletters.com and tell them Spalutions sent you!

Constant Contact – Online Marketing made easy through email marketing, polls, surveys and event invitations. Get a free 30 day trial at http://www.constantcontact.com/index.jsp?pn=spalutions

Shelene Taylor/ IAMBIZ.com -   I recommend Shelene to any wellness professional who wants to improve their prosperity and profitability though her Money Mindset Breakthrough Program. Learn more at: http://www.1shoppingcart.com/app/?af=1476284

ABOUT THE AUTHOR

Felicia Brown, LMBT is the owner of Spa*lutions!*, (www.spalutions.com) and provides business and marketing coaching for massage, spa and wellness professionals. She is passionate about inspiring others and has a personal philosophy and practice of sharing her knowledge and experience with others so that they may become successful in all of their endeavors. Felicia's practice of "cooperative competition" has been a cornerstone of her career since becoming a massage therapist in 1994.

Felicia has won many awards for her business acumen and industry involvement including: **2011 Volunteer of the Year** (*American Massage Conference*); **2009 Spa Person of the Year** (*Day Spa Association*); **2005 Small Business Person of the Year** (*Greensboro Chamber of Commerce*); **Top Entrepreneurs of 2009/Top 25 Movers & Shakers of 2008** (*Business Leader Magazine*), **2007 National Volunteer Committee of the Year** (*American Massage Therapy Association*), **2004 Women in Business** (*The Business Journal*); & **2003 Forty Leaders Under Forty** (*The Business Journal*).

This is Felicia's first book. Since the first edition came out, she has also published *Reflections of My Heart: A Poetic Journey of Love, Life, Heartbreak and Healing* and has contributed to numerous other industry publications and books. Her third book *The Sunflower Princess: A Healing Fairy Tale* will be available in October 2014. Her blog, www.ZenVersusZin.com documents her journey of exploring sobriety and is the "pre-quel" to her planned book of the same name which is due out in 2015.

Felicia makes her home in Greensboro, NC. In her spare time, Felicia is a casually competitive tri-athlete and also enjoys yoga, reading, cooking, travel, and spa/travel adventures of most any sort.

OTHER PRODUCTS

 Need clarity on what you're trying to do or accomplish? **Build your foundation with this CD.** Improve your skills, confidence and effectiveness in marketing through this audio CD - GOAL SETTING. In it you' l learn how to: Get a clear picture of what you want in your life and business; Find the time for achieving your dreams; Gain confidence in your talents, abilities and business skills; Set specific, quantifiable realistic goals; Determine the steps and tasks needed to achieve your personal and professional goals.

 All of the meditations on this CD are original, but they have been inspired by the words and work of many including Louise Hay, Caroline Myss, Wayne Dyer, Marianne Williamson and Shakti Gawain and by my thousands of students and clients. I hope you will use **Just Breathe** with your own clients and students. It is perfect as a pre-treatment relaxation in massage therapy sessions and nail treatments, a meditative add-on during facial or body masks or an end of yoga class cool down.

 In <u>Retailing for Massage, Spa & Salon Pros</u>, you'll get specific **strategies on how to ethically improve your retailing mindset, confidence, skills and results.** Specifically you'll learn: Why people don't sell retail; Why consumers buy retail; How to effectively sell products; Tips for strong retail sales; and how to add a product line or vendor

 **Events created without planning are not likely to bring in many visitors, generate media interest or add extra sales.** This detailed guide will help you prepare for many successful events in your business.

Order these products at www.Spalutions.com or www.EveryTouchMarketing.com.

FREE PREVIEW

Free & Easy Ways to Promote Your Massage, Spa or Wellness Business

Volume 2: Creating Lifetime Clients

CREATING LIFETIME CLIENTS

In Volume 1, I wrote that marketing is everything that "touches" a client and makes them want to come to you the first time, the next time, or perhaps the last time. It's every interaction that you have with a client, whether it's you personally, or it's your business card, or your voicemail, or your website or whatever.

As we've also discussed, when we're talking about getting clients to rebook and creating lifetime clients, it's important for us to understand why it is that they come to us in the first place. A lot of people think they have a definition of why people come in and get massage or why they want facials, or why they come to a spa, but essentially it's a combination of things.

It could be they want to improve their health and well-being, they're there to decrease their pain and discomfort, they want to escape from stress, they want to be restored and renewed, have peace and quiet, and maybe they just want just a little mini vacation. In the case of skin-care they may have specific beauty or aging concerns that they're looking to address. Or on the wellness side, they may want to feel better or live a healthier lifestyle.

Unfortunately, if we haven't communicated with clients properly before or during their first or subsequent visits, things can be confusing, scary, overwhelming and even disappointing. Think about how you would feel if you didn't know what was going to happen when you had a bikini wax, or if you didn't know you had to get undressed to get on the massage table and that everything about the appointment was a surprise to you.

All kinds of things can make a visit for a massage or a facial, or any other treatment, less than what the client had hoped for. Some people end up feeling frustrated or tired, or they think that the price they paid - no matter what it was - was too expensive or not a good value. The bottom line is they can end up feeling stressed as a result of us not catering to their needs.

As caring professionals who want to cultivate rapport and long-term relationships with our clients we want to make sure that that doesn't happen. So to do the very best we can to create an amazing experience and get the clients to want to come back, we want to, try and anticipate their client's needs before they arise.

One example: In my treatment room I keep a robe on the door, in case someone might have to use the bathroom in the middle of their session so they won't have to get dressed again.

Something else I do since my office can be difficult to find is to email them specific, descriptive directions to the office as soon as they book their appointment. To save time in case they get lost, I also send them a client intake form to print and fill out before their appointment. I also send email appointment reminders to all my clients each and every week about 24 hours before the appointment. They know they can count on the reminder so they're not unexpectedly missing an appointment.

Basically, I try to see things through my client's eyes. A coating of dust I might overlook if it were in my home but in my office I really try to make sure it never really builds up. I also work to keep my processes smooth and consistent so that is always doing things the same way. Also, of course being understanding, flexible, and helpful; always working to make things better and providing what I call custom service for clients. In other words, really giving people what it is that helps them feel like their taken care of.

In addition to this, I do whatever I can to make each of my clients feel special and cared for in ways that matter to them. I have one client who adores the fact that I keep Wintergreen LifeSavers in my treatment room and bathroom for her. She loves them so much that

I also decorate the table with them in a different design every time she comes in. I do that for her because she loves them and she gets a kick out of the effort I make.

I have another client that really likes Tootsie Rolls so I keep Tootsie Rolls in my office for her and make sure to put a couple on the table before each of her appointments. Other people that really like hot towels and aromatherapy so they get both. Others prefer a cool room and no blanket when they come in. Some folks like a bolster under their feet and some that like a pillow. Remembering these things and providing those clients with what suits them best helps me to set myself apart from other therapists. It also turns people into lifetime clients and makes every visit with me all that much better.

So, I want you take a minute and just think about your favorite spa, massage, spa or other wellness service experience ever. It could be a massage experience or your favorite facial, it doesn't really matter. Take a moment to write down answers to these three questions:

What exactly made that experience so special?

_____

_____

What is it that stands out in your mind about that experience?

_____

_____

Why did you want to go back again?

_____

_____

_____

Go to www.EveryTouchMarketing.com for details

48357609R00084

Made in the USA
San Bernardino, CA
23 April 2017